BRICK
BY
BRICK

ADVANCE PRAISE FOR THE BOOK

'*Brick by Brick* stands as a testament to Manish's unwavering commitment to support fellow entrepreneurs. I've always marvelled at his desire to share knowledge and foster growth within the entrepreneurial community. This book is yet another remarkable effort in that direction. It's an essential read for anyone on the journey to building their dreams'—**Aman Gupta, co-founder and chief marketing officer, boAt Lifestyle**

'From building a wall in the scorching heat of Haryana to architecting multiple successful tech ventures, Manish Vij's entrepreneurial journey embodies grit, serendipity and the transformative power of dreams. A masterclass in building businesses, *Brick by Brick* is testament to how middle-class values, combined with unwavering perseverance, can create extraordinary impact'—**Ankur Warikoo, entrepreneur**

'Some remarkable entrepreneurial lessons weaved into an anecdotal and relatable narrative that keeps the pages turning. Humorous yet profound stories, which can only come from growing up in India, take you down memory lane with Manish while you cannot help but reminisce about your own journey. A must-read!'—**Anupam Mittal, founder and chief executive officer, People Group**

'*Brick by Brick* unpacks the entrepreneurial journey with practical lessons and real-world experiences. It offers budding entrepreneurs a candid look at the challenges and opportunities of building a business, emphasizing resilience, adaptability and execution. At its heart, the book reminds us that entrepreneurship is about consistent effort and turning ideas into impact, one step at a time'—**Deep Kalra, founder and chairman, MakeMyTrip**

'This book reflects Manish's inspiring journey of growth and leadership; his first decade as a founder incubated within Smile Group and now as a partner giving back to the community'—**Harish Bahl, founder and chairman, Smile Group**

'Manish's *Brick by Brick* is a masterclass in resilience and grit, offering readers a candid glimpse into the challenges and triumphs of entrepreneurship. With actionable insights and heartfelt anecdotes, it inspires dreamers to build their vision, one brick at a time. A must-read for aspiring entrepreneurs and leaders alike'—**Kunal Bahl, co-founder, Titan Capital and Snapdeal**

'Manish has tracked India's Internet arc longer than anyone else I know. His story is that of grit and passion and must be read by all aspiring entrepreneurs'—**Paras Chopra, founder and chairman, Wingify**

'*Brick by Brick* is an exceptional guide for every aspiring entrepreneur. The book lays down an essential road map with unmatched clarity and insight. A must-read for anyone looking to navigate the entrepreneurial landscape and build their dreams from the ground up'—**Sanjeev Bikhchandani, founder and executive vice chairman, Info Edge**

'On the one hand, you have theorists of entrepreneurship who wish their theories are put into practice; on the other, you have practitioners' accounts which grapple with a general theorization of individual experiences. Manish Vij's account straddles both worlds seamlessly. He seems to have learnt and internalized the practice of entrepreneurship while simultaneously trying to put a theoretical framework around it. Great read'—**Dr Subho Ray, president, Internet and Mobile Association of India**

'We both come from a middle-class background, and in Manish's incredible story, you will find inspiration for building great success. All the hustle and hard work, a joyful anecdotal read. With sincere hardwork and determination, you can achieve your dreams. Instead of your background, your commitment needs to be perfect'—**Vijay Shekhar Sharma, founder, One97 and Paytm**

'Manish is smart, sharp and full of life. He's been that way for as long as I've known him, over twenty years. This isn't a preachy book; it's an honest, must-read for founders and aspiring founders. It brings to life so many characters and stories. Along the way, you'll find golden nuggets of wisdom. If it feels right, the business is thriving and the future looks bright, just go for it. I love the simplicity of it all'—**Yashish Dahiya, chairman and chief executive officer, PB Fintech Limited**

BRICK BY BRICK

From **Middle-Class Roots**
to **Entrepreneurial Success**

A Road Map to Dream,
Build and Succeed

MANISH VIJ

PENGUIN
BUSINESS

An imprint of Penguin Random House

PENGUIN BUSINESS

Penguin Business is an imprint of the Penguin Random House group of companies whose
addresses can be found at global.penguinrandomhouse.com

Published by Penguin Random House India Pvt. Ltd
4th Floor, Capital Tower 1, MG Road,
Gurugram 122 002, Haryana, India

First published in Penguin Business by Penguin Random House India 2025

ISBN 9780143473275

Typeset in Adobe Garamond Pro by MAP Systems, Bengaluru, India
Printed at Replika Press Pvt. Ltd, India

www.penguin.co.in

Contents

Introduction

'Is there really any need for another book on entrepreneurship?'—this was the question I posed to myself when the thought of penning my entrepreneurial journey first raised its head. I certainly didn't want to write because I harboured any dreams of becoming a bestselling author; neither did I want to use the book as a PR tool to build a personal brand. Of course, I was instrumental in creating some disruptive businesses, but other entrepreneurs had far greater successes. Why tell my story then? Each time I asked myself this question, the answer that I received was this—'My story is proof that the power of a dream and its relentless execution can get you far.' Coming from a middle-class background, that is all I had—an audacious dream. 'If I can fulfil my dream, others can too,' I heard myself say. The book is simply born out of this desire to share some of the insights from the entrepreneurial trenches in the hope that many others could benefit from them. *Brick by Brick* is not just a catchy title but an apt summarization of the importance of a gradual and incremental approach towards achieving your dreams—something that I undertook for twenty-five years of my life

The one thing I have observed is that while young people are awed by entrepreneurial success stories, many of the entrepreneurial challenges tend to be overlooked. Beneath the glitz and glamour of entrepreneurship, it is the ability to show up every single day that makes miracles happen. Therefore, in telling my story I didn't just want to recount the large funding rounds we had received or our much-hyped exits. What I wanted to do was to assess what led me to these successes as also the mistakes that I made along the way. As you read the book, you will notice that I have followed up the key milestones of my journey with actionable insights that I feel could be of value to aspiring entrepreneurs. It is no coincidence that these insights ask you to DARE—**D**ream larger than life, take relentless and focused **A**ction, build lasting **R**elationships and be open to making the most of the serendipitous **E**dge that life has to offer you.

Think of this book then as that little nudge that could help you as you chart your entrepreneurial journey. My prayer for you is that you stay curious throughout this ride; and as you scale newer heights, you keep paying it forward. This book is also a humble effort in that direction.

Entrepreneurship is set to play a crucial role in India's journey towards becoming a multi-trillion-dollar economy. If this book can help even a few aspiring entrepreneurs enhance or shorten their learning curve, I will have fulfilled the purpose with which I set out to write it.

Chapter 1

Your Concern Is One Brick

'Bhaiya, ye deewar toot-ti kyun nahi?'

There is an advertisement that most of us have grown up watching. It shows a horde of people trying to break down a wall—*'beech ki deewar'*—that was constructed in the middle of a house by two brothers. Amidst their dramatic reconciliation, they try hard to demolish the wall but fail miserably and ultimately give up. It turns out that real life works differently from reel life. In real life, the wall whose construction I was painstakingly overseeing had been broken down by someone in no time at all.

It was the month of May; the state of Haryana had declared the onset of a heatwave with temperatures rising to over 45 degrees. Yet here I was, all of sixteen years old, standing in the midst of an open field every single day supervising the construction of a wall. For some reason, just as I had finished my Class XI exams, my father had decided that it was time for me to head to Gohana, a small town in Haryana, where my grandparents and extended family lived. Even before I could jump up with joy at the thought of a pampered vacation, my father had pronounced his judgement. *'Tumhe hamari zameen ke aas pass ek deewar banwani hai* (You have to get a wall built around our land).' The said 'zameen' was among a few of the land parcels that were allocated to my grandparents when they had landed in India after the partition, to begin life afresh as 'refugees'. Often referred to as 'bhatte ki zameen', this was not agricultural land but one where bricks were manufactured. My grandparents had painstakingly converted that land into arable land and had many emotions associated with it.

Not allowing something as small as a wall to come in the way of an exciting summer break, I had nodded in assent at my father's suggestion. It was only when I reached Gohana that I realized what I had signed up for. While my father had appointed a contractor to do the job, my first task was to accompany him in the summer heat to ensure that the right bricks were bought. Thereafter, it was back-breaking work to stand in the scorching sun for long hours, day after day, to supervise the workers laying the bricks. That a summer break came with no weekends or holidays was disappointing, especially as I saw my cousins lazing around all day. For the life of me, I could not imagine why my father had decided to punish me.

It was only as the wall started coming up, brick by brick, that I began to feel the beginnings of a sense of purpose, of ownership and pride, at giving shape to my first independent project. As the wall grew in size, I also began to feel a sense of awe towards the workers who were working relentlessly, putting one brick over the other. They were demonstrating that a goal, no matter how big or complex, simply required you to show up every single day and keep performing small tasks consistently.

One morning though, I was in for a rude shock. As I walked into the field, I was devastated to see a part of the wall lying broken. The way the bricks were strewn all over, it was clear that someone had forcibly brought the wall down. That I was furious, is an understatement. On asking around, I was told that it was the work of one of our relatives, who owned the adjoining piece of land. I remember barging into his house only to find that if I was angry, he was angrier. '*Tumne zameen galat naapi hai* (You have erred in measuring the land),' he yelled, as soon as he sighted me. It turned out that in making the measurements, I had made an error, and the wall had trespassed into his field by a few centimetres. Looking back, I think I learnt important lessons in failure, people handling and negotiation that day. It was only when I was able to address his complaint and convince him that the error was not intentional that he allowed me to resume the project again.

By this time, the project had become a personal obsession of sorts for me, one that I had to finish. I distinctly recall that hot June afternoon when the workers finally pronounced the wall as 'ready'. 'We have done it,' I remember proudly exclaiming to my father over a phone call. His reaction though was one that I couldn't have ever anticipated. While he congratulated me on a project well done, to my utter surprise, he informed me that we were in the process of selling that piece of land.

Several times in my adult life, I have wondered if the construction of that wall was required at all, since my father had made up his mind to sell the plot of land. Each time I was led to the conclusion that my father had wanted to teach me some early life lessons—of persistence, integrity, showing up every single day, weathering adversity and a lot more. Come to think of it, Project Wall also turned out to be my first lesson in building my hustling muscle, one that would come in very handy in later life.

The story of the wall would be incomplete without a mention of a rather serendipitous event that took place only recently. Sometime in early 2022, I was travelling for work, when the face of Will Smith, the iconic Hollywood actor, stared at me from the cover of his newly released autobiography which was on display in a bookshop at New Delhi airport. Imagine my utter surprise when I was greeted by an early chapter called 'The Wall'. In this chapter, Will Smith talks about how his father put the eleven-year-old Will and his younger brother to work, to build a new wall in front of his shop. He goes on to describe how every day for nearly a year, he and his brother went to his father's shop after school to work on that wall, mixing the mortar themselves and laying the bricks. As days went by, they began to feel totally hopeless in the face of the enormity of the job. Just as they were ready to give up the seemingly never-ending project, their father's life-changing advice altered their mindsets. 'Stop thinking of the damn wall!' his father exclaimed. 'There is no wall. There are only bricks. Your job is to lay this brick perfectly. Then move on to the next brick. Don't be worrying about no wall. Your concern is one brick.' Smith goes on to recount how that one lesson not only helped them to finish the wall, it also changed their lives. The secret to success, Smith says, is 'as boring as it is unsurprising.' You simply show up and lay another brick. 'Pissed off? Lay another brick. Bad opening weekend? Lay another brick. Album sales dropping? Lay another brick,' he recounts eloquently.

It is uncanny how parents separated by continents think of similar ways to instil early life lessons in their children!

Actionable Insights

Show up every single day: In my experience, one of the biggest markers of success—whether in your health, career or just about any other life goal—is to show up consistently. It is important to remind yourself that anything that you haven't done before inevitably seems hard at first. It takes time to get comfortable with it, turn it into a habit and then into a state of joy. Entrepreneurship, for instance, is quite like climbing a mountain. There will be enough and more times when inspiration will fade and you will find yourself struggling. Climb the mountain at your own speed; take breaks enroute if you need to, but just don't give up.

Enjoy the process: When you start climbing a mountain, you want to quickly reach the peak. The important thing, however, is to enjoy the beauty around you as you take each step towards your goal. Psychological studies on goal setting have also gone on to show that focusing on the inputs, rather than the outcome, tends to reduce stress and improve performance. So go ahead and enjoy the process while also celebrating those small milestones. The rewards could be as small as ringing a bell on achieving a daily target or a team samosa party on successfully developing a product feature.

In closing, remember that showing up is half the battle won; staying committed is the rest!

Chapter 2

An Unusual Workstation

'Aaj bhi truck jana hai, sir? (Will the truck go today as well, sir?)' I was asked by the Public Call Office (PCO) booth operator, a young enthusiastic chap, who was about my age. That he was happy to encounter a high-value customer was evident in his smile. This wasn't the first time that he had tried to strike up a conversation with me. On other occasions, I would end up spending a few extra minutes responding to his many questions. Today, however, I barely had time to nod and get to the business at hand before rushing in to attend a Business Management class where the professor was a stickler for punctuality.

I had started flexing my entrepreneurial muscle from a rather unusual workspace. A PCO booth—those yellow kiosks that had at one time ushered in a communication revolution in the country—was the seat of my early entrepreneurial journey. Come to think of it, today's generation may not have even heard of their existence, let alone seen them stand on street corners, not when everyone carries a phone in their pocket, anyway.

I had only recently been packed off to the city of Indore from Delhi, which had been my family's home for decades. I was to pursue a course in business management at a time when business education was just making an appearance on the scene. These were times when every student worth his salt aspired for a seat at the prestigious Indian Institute of Technology (IIT) or a good medical college. An average student, I had also given the entrance exam a shot (and failed at it) as a rite of passage. Fortunately for me, my parents were far-sighted enough to see that it was time for me to cut my losses and try my hand at something different.

When it came to my father's notice that his friend, Mr Khandelia, who was working as the CEO of a large spinning mill, was sending his son, Ashish, a bright student, to Indore for a course in business management, he decided that I should follow suit. It was on the Malwa Express enroute to the International Institute of Professional Studies at the Devi Ahilya University in Indore that I first met Ashish who was to be my partner in crime for the next few years. We were to be picked up at Dewas station by Ashish's uncle, Ashok Chacha. While I was a bit nervous, stepping out of home for the first time, I soon realized that my fears were unfounded. Ashok Chacha, a textile mill owner in Dewas, and his wife, Kanta Chachi, welcomed me with open arms and over a period of time, became my extended family.

Yarn Trading

'*Ek business opportunity hai; tere paas time hai karne ke liye* (There is a business opportunity; do you have time to pursue it)?'

This question from my father, on our weekly long-distance call from Indore, had sparked an old hustling muscle in me.

A textile engineer by profession, my father had spent his entire working life in the textile industry. He had harboured entrepreneurial ambitions at a time when entrepreneurship wasn't as cool and shiny as it is today. His early attempts to put up a yarn spinning plant had caused him to lose a lot of money but hadn't prevented him from continuing to hone an entrepreneurial mindset. Driven by his fervour, I had also spent a large part of my school vacations accompanying him as he visited various textile plants. My early interest in the industry had even led me to undertake summer training in a textile factory in Sangrur, Punjab, at a time when summer internships weren't as regimented as they are now.

My old interest in entrepreneurship was reignited. Within minutes of my father posing the question, I found myself ready to turn into an entrepreneur from the very PCO booth from which I had made a call to him. It turned out that my father was friends with someone who ran a spinning mill in Nepal, a man who was keen to export yarn to India. He also happened to know a few potential buyers in Ludhiana who were keen to buy their goods. All that was needed was someone who could reliably liaison between the two parties. A few statistics from my father and I had already made a quick calculation that I could stand to make as much as Rs 8000 for every truckload that made its way from Nepal to Ludhiana. Even if I ended up coordinating two to three trucks a month, we were still talking about a lot of money.

The amount seemed princely, especially if I compared it with the Rs 1200-odd that I received from home every month to manage my expenses, of which a sizable Rs 700 was the mess fee alone. Of course, the money wouldn't come to me, but the thought that it would help pay my college fees was comforting.

Over the next few years, I spent many fruitful hours at the PCO, making calls and coordinating orders between Nepal and Ludhiana, between my many business management classes. While my professors were leaving no stone unturned in teaching us the building blocks of business, here I was learning the nuances of a profit and loss statement, hands-on. After the initial excitement of making money subsided a little, I realized that for every Rs 8000 that the successful delivery of a truck offered me, the truck itself was valued at over Rs 8 lakh. Any lapse in coordination could cost me dearly. While I did make mistakes along the way, fortunately for me, I could manage them myself without having to bring them to the notice of my father. What I learnt in the bargain were some real management skills.

It was this early brush with success that led me to think of several other entrepreneurial projects. From dreaming of setting up a chain of highway dhabas (food outlets) to setting up a factory that manufactured pouches for selling mineral water, my mind was brimming with ideas and my notebooks with business plans (these were pre-PowerPoint days!). Each time I ran into the same roadblock—I had no capital to invest. So strong, however, was this zeal to earn an additional income that I just wouldn't relent. Sure enough, this relentless thinking soon led me to an idea that could be executed without making a significant investment.

Project Uniform

Indore was home to a number of industrial plants. While hunting for ideas, I noticed that workers of large industrial plants were dressed in immaculate uniforms. Workers of mid-sized and smaller plants, however, did not have this luxury. I instinctively knew that I had hit upon an opportunity. So strong was my conviction that almost every single day after classes would end, my friend, Ajit Kaushal, and I would travel over an hour to Pitampur industrial area to cold-call industrial plants. It helped that I had, by then, struck a deal with someone who ran a shop selling cloth and uniforms in the main bazaar of Indore. It turned out that he was equally entrepreneurial, and even gave me his old Maruti van to make it easy for us to travel. That it helped me spin another business model is the subject of another story, as I used the van to offer a ride to passengers at the rate of Rs 20 a person, making money in the bargain to pay for the fuel and even ending up saving a few bucks! That apart, the van came in handy as I could cold-call several admin/HR personnel of industrial plants each day, explaining the many advantages of having uniforms for workers and how we could help them procure the uniforms on a cost-efficient basis.

'You have a deal!'

That one sentence still rings in my ears—perhaps even
sweeter than the many multimillion dollar deals that I have
subsequently struck in my career. We were at one of India's
largest auto manufacturers, making a long-winded pitch to their
HR head, until he cut us short and agreed to place an order for
some 2000-odd uniforms. In that one moment, I truly felt that
the world was at my feet. The hour-long journey back to the
campus didn't seem half as tedious, filled as I was with so much
hope. Looking back, I can safely say that those years and those
early successes took away any fear of dreaming big from me,
which is really the starting point of any journey, no matter how
audacious it may seem at the time.

Actionable Insights

Hunger drives success: There are enough and more stories that we have heard where erstwhile prosperous families have declined in the lifetime of their third or fourth generations. The first generation, the wealth creators, work hard; the second generation—mostly because it has seen the first-generation struggle to build—works equally hard to grow. The third generation maintains the wealth and the fourth generation often destroys it. The same holds true for companies. This is no coincidence. The reason, at the risk of generalizing, is the lack of hunger in the subsequent generations.

The commonly used phrase, 'fire in the belly' truly stands for being 'hungry' which, in turn, drives relentless action and therefore success.

Dream—Deal—Do it (D-D-D): People are often conditioned to think that lack of resources, especially money, is the biggest barrier to their dream. I grew up believing it too. What we do not take into account is that there are people and institutions, in India and the world, who have the requisite capital and are on the lookout for people who have dreams and have a bias towards action. With the world being well connected, we may at best have 'three degrees of separation' from them. Instead of focusing on lack of resources then, you will do well to focus on D-D-D—the dream, the 'do it' attitude and the deal with potential capital providers.

Find a mentor to accelerate your success: Both popular fiction as well as the business landscape are full of stories where a significant part of the protagonist's success can be attributed to a mentor figure who offers the right counsel and guidance. Mentors / coaches are actually quite badass. They are wise, they understand what your limiting beliefs are and importantly, they show up in times of great trouble and can give directions to your efforts. Remember Gandalf and his iconic line, 'You shall not pass' in *The Lord of the Rings*?

While you may have different mentors at every stage of your life, based on the personal and professional growth you seek, it is important to find a mentor who is invested in you through love and/or capital, as the case may be.

In closing, remember that strength does not come from what you can do; it comes from overcoming the things you once thought you couldn't.

Chapter 3

KabadiBazaar

Launching a start-up to land a job!

Yes, crazy as it may sound, my sole aim in launching my first start-up was to land a job! Growing up as a middle-class boy in the India of the 1990s when entrepreneurship wasn't a thing yet, all I cared for was to get a stable job with a decent pay cheque. Given that academics was not my strength, I knew that it would be hard for me to compete with my peers and crack those campus placement interviews. I was conscious of the fact that I had to make my resumé count to be offered a job!

'Tujhe pata hai Internet karke ek cheez hai (Have you heard of something called the Internet)?' My roommate Ashish Khandelia, with whom I had undertaken the journey to Indore, asked me one morning. An early tech adopter, Ashish was the first in our college to own a laptop. It was a Compaq laptop that we had carefully stowed inside the locker of the lone steel almirah in our room. 'Young people are doing business on the Internet,' he went on to explain, pulling up an issue of an international business magazine to validate his point. The magazine had carried a story on how hotel bookings could now be made in a few clicks using the power of the Internet. 'Let us study this model a little in detail,' he said excitedly. Subsequently, we visited a few hotels in Indore to conduct a pilot study on whether hotel owners would be interested in

collaborating with us if we created a website that facilitated bookings for them. Before we could go any further, however, Ashish cleared his chartered accountancy (CA) exams and was all set to give his career a new direction. His exit from the campus was a huge reality check for me. The only support that I had once Ashish left was the kindness of Ashok Chacha and Kanta Chachi, who continued to be as loving and caring towards me. Not only would they come to meet me regularly, they also made sure that each time I crossed Dewas station, on board the Intercity Express from Indore to Delhi, a homecooked meal awaited me. It was the love that they showered on me that made the rest of my stay in Indore so comfortable. I was now determined to make the remaining year and a half, before my course ended, count.

'*Yaar, hamara resumé extracurricular mein hi ban sakta hai* (We can make a resumé out of our extracurricular activities alone),' I remember telling my other roommate, Rohit Kanthra, as both of us put together an audacious plan to start an 'industry–institute interface' programme under the placement committee of the college. The programme helped us to become the faces of the institute and reach out to industry leaders, to invite them to speak to students at the campus. Our goal was twofold—to improve the brand value of the college and build a network to be able to secure a summer training and job for ourselves. We invited corporate leaders from companies such as ACC, IBM, Bridgestone, etc. as a part of the programme. The plan worked to an extent; I bagged a summer internship with IBM thanks to the direct interface with a guest speaker from the company.

I knew, however, that it wouldn't be easy to get a job this way and that I had to work on my start-up idea quickly in order to differentiate my resumé from those of the other bright students in college.

Internet to the rescue

The one thing that stayed with me after Ashish left was the fact that he had said that it is easy to transact business on the Internet. It was this feverish desire to do something that woke me at 2 a.m. and compelled me to write a business idea and a plan. I had finally found a problem statement and a winning idea that could be showcased at my placement interview. I decided to build a classified website that would allow users to connect with each other and trade second-hand items.

Of course, to my job-focused mind, it wasn't enough to come up with an idea. I also had to execute it if I wanted a recruiter to see value in me. The search for someone to code the website led me to Ashwani Mehta, a topper in the institute's Masters of Computer Application (MCA) course. I approached him with the idea and requested him to partner with me. Ashwani, however, wasn't open to a partnership and made it clear that the coding would come at a cost. A quick calculation put the total project cost at Rs 75,000, a whopping figure for a student back in 1999. A senior, Sumeet Mehta, came to my rescue at this time. Having recently secured a job, he agreed to turn co-founder and invest Rs 20,000. Encouraged by his 'Vij, *tu kar lega* (Vij, you can do it),' I reached out to my father with a request to invest the remaining Rs 55,000, turning him into my first investor, without him receiving any equity.

That accomplished, it was time to purchase a domain name that would cost me another Rs 2000-odd, a sizable part of my seed capital. This led to the birth of www.kabadibazaar.com, a name inspired by the *kabadi wala*, the unorganized small-time scrap dealer who periodically visits Indian households and buys unwanted goods.

In about four to five months, we were ready with the website. With no money to spend on advertising, the next big challenge I faced was to promote the website so that I could drive traffic towards it. It didn't help that I was left with barely Rs 10,000 out of the Rs 75,000 that I had raised; advertising the website was therefore out of the question. It so happened that I was in the college mess one day, when the television was playing a story about the dot-com boom and how upcoming websites were promising to change the world. 'If only *KabadiBazaar* could also be covered by the media,' I remember thinking to myself. Not one to waste a good idea, I quickly pulled up a tissue lying around and jotted down a list of the top newspapers, TV channels, radio stations and magazines that I could approach.

My first pit stop was at *Dainik Jagran*, a popular newspaper in Indore. I remember marching into their office and requesting to see a news reporter. While they entertained my request, when I requested the reporter to write about my website in his newspaper, his answer was a nonchalant *'Aise kaise likh dein* (How can we just go ahead and write about it)?' I asked him what he meant, and his answer was *'Isme kahani kya hai* (What is the story here)?' It was then that I realized that for a story to be carried in the media, it requires what is known as a 'news peg'. I supplied that, by telling him that I was the youngest person in my college to have started this website. That struck him as being interesting.

The story made it to the newspaper and spoke about how an Indore lad had brought fame to the city by launching an innovative website. Besides giving the website traction in Indore, the coverage also fulfilled my basic aim—uplifting my status in college!

I had now tasted blood. I decided to venture beyond Indore to get some additional publicity for the website. There couldn't be a better place than heading back home to Delhi. This time, encouraged by my early success, I decided to knock on the doors of the *Times of India*. 'The story has already been covered. There is nothing new for us to write about,' the journalist there said to me, much to my disappointment. The response, although negative, led me to yet another insight. I now decided to approach news production houses and news channels, as they would have the first mover advantage in the television medium. It was a cold call at the NDTV office that got me my big break. As luck would have it, Nidhi Razdan, who was covering the tech beat for NDTV, was interested in the story. The next thing I knew was that Nidhi, along with her crew, was coming home to interview me. That my entire West Delhi neighbourhood was excited to see a television crew in their backyard is an understatement.

By the time the coverage was aired, I was back at my hostel in Indore. This time sitting in the same mess, it was surreal to watch yet another Internet success story on TV—mine! The national coverage worked and how! Not only did the traffic on the website begin to increase day by the day, people were also beginning to buy and sell products.

Emboldened by this success, I decided to double down and once again go back to The *Times of India* with yet another idea for a headline story—the fact that I was in very early talks with another classified website for a potential acquisition by kabadibazaar. While the acquisition didn't happen, the *Times of India* saw a news peg in the story. Based on it, the journalist concerned got the necessary approvals to carry it on the front page of the newspaper. On the day the story was to be carried, I was over the moon. There was no way I could wait till the early hours of the morning for the newspaper to be delivered to my house. I decided to ask my best friend, Deven Dharamdasani, to accompany me to the

Times of India office at 3 a.m., to lay our hands on the first printed copy of the newspaper. After all that effort, imagine my dejection when on scanning not just the front page but the entire newspaper, we didn't find any mention of KabadiBazaar. I was heartbroken since I had already imagined the headline and the huge validation it would be for my efforts. You could cut the tense air with a knife as we drove back home in absolute silence.

If the night seemed bleak, a phone call the next morning once again filled me with hope. 'I am sorry the story couldn't be carried today because of some last-minute coverage. It will be carried tomorrow, don't worry,' I was told by the journalist concerned. Our trip to the TOI office in the dead of the night this time was filled with anticipation. 'Deven, *tu dekh* (Deven, you check),' I handed over the newspaper to my friend, hoping to break the jinx of last night. No sooner had he held the paper than I heard him shout with delight. '*Tu toh chha gaya*, Manish (You have done it, Manish),' he said, hugging me tight. As I stared at the headline tears filled my eyes. It felt unreal that the newspaper I had grown up reading was telling my story to the world. Armed with a copy of the paper, I was so excited that I could hardly drive the car back home. The world seemed to be at my feet. In my excitement, I parked the car on the side of the road and sat down on the pavement at that unearthly hour. 'I have achieved a lot.. If I die today, it is fine,' I told Deven, overwhelmed with emotion.

KabadiBazaar subsequently saw a lot more coverage in mainstream newspapers and magazines, driving a lot of visitors to the website with zero marketing cost. In today's parlance this would possibly be referred to as a 'growth hack'. I was living my dream. All this turned me into a hero of sorts not just among my peers, but also among my professors who now saw me in a whole new light, far removed from the marks that I was securing. By this time, the website was also showing increased traffic with over 100 queries on the site every day

A Legal Case and an Injunction

The growing popularity of KabadiBazaar took my story not just to the front pages of newspapers and magazines but also to a very unlikely destination, the High Court.

While I was purchasing the domain name for the website, my budget had allowed me to purchase only one domain name—www.kabadibazaar.com. I was not able to book related domain names, as was the practice, so as to dissuade other people from purchasing and misusing them. I was to pay a price for that omission.

It so happened that a certain Mrs Indra Chugh (and her husband) had purchased around twenty to thirty domain names surrounding mine, including the very close www.kabaribazaar. com (replacing d with r). This was leading to a lot of traffic being diverted to their website. Some press stories also ended up mentioning their website. These were early days in the dot-com journey and intelligent search engines had not yet made an appearance, further exacerbating the issue.

I decided to reach out to the owners of this domain name, only to realize that they were in the business of farming domain names and were unwilling to relent. I didn't know what to do. It was at this time that someone counselled me that while I didn't have a trademark, since I had registered a domain name, it amounted to an IP of sorts. I was told that the best IP law firm in the country was Anand and Anand, and that it would be in my interest to approach them. For someone who had never as much as been to a court before, all this was absolutely alien territory. Nonetheless, I decided to take the bull by the horns. It so happened that the office of Anand and Anand was located at Nizamuddin in New Delhi, not far away from the Nizamuddin railway station where the Intercity Express from Indore arrived. I decided to head to their office immediately from the railway station, only to realize that I was over three hours early since the office opened only at 10 a.m.

As soon as the clock ticked past 10 am, the office opened and the receptionist made her way to her work desk. She was greeted by a travel weary guy, who had just stepped down from his second-class sleeper bogie, a suitcase in tow, and who wanted to meet senior lawyer Pravin Anand, the Managing Partner of the firm. 'Do you have an appointment?' she asked, surprise written large all over her face. On hearing my

monosyllabic 'no', she tried to reason with me that Pravin
Anand did not meet anyone without a prior appointment.
There was perhaps a steely resolve in me; that, coupled with
the fact that I had been waiting patiently for over three hours,
prompted her to hear my entire story. On listening to me,
she very kindly offered to get me to meet Safir Anand, Pravin
Anand's brother, also a respected lawyer who had a knack
for technology.. On hearing my story, he asked me to come
back in the evening when Pravin Anand was also likely to
be in office.

I made the trip to Nizamuddin once again in the evening
and this time was guided to meet Mr Pravin Anand. '*Haan,
bacche, batao, kya hua* (Okay, son, tell me, what happened)?'
I was comforted by his warm voice as soon as I entered his
huge, rather intimidating office located on the top floor of the
building. On narrating my predicament, he immediately called
in some other lawyers of his team who also had a strong tech
orientation.

After all of them had heard my story, Mr Anand put a
young promising lawyer, Neel Mason, on the case and asked
him to start preparing a file. It was when the meeting drew to
a close that I sheepishly walked up to Mr Anand to tell him
that I had no money to pay his fee. '*Fee zindagi mein phir kabhi*
(I'll take the fee sometime later in life), for now let us win,' Mr
Anand said, while patting my back, leaving me in awe of this
senior lawyer who was under no obligation to help me. Not

only did I have no money to pay his fee, I had also not come to him with any reference. Come to think of it, it was sheer grit or perhaps a large amount of stubbornness that had led me to the office of the largest IP law firm, unannounced.

I was informed by Mr Anand that while the case was tough as I did not have any registered trademark, they would try their best and file for an injunction in the High Court. On the appointed date, I witnessed Mr Anand's aura first-hand in court as he made an impressive representation to the honourable judge replete with all the case laws. When it was time for the judge to pronounce his verdict, I literally felt as if I had my heart in my mouth. My relief knew no bounds when we were granted an ex parte injunction that ordered that all the surrounding domain names around KabadiBazaar had to be shut down. I still recall the triumphant smile on Mr Anand's face on hearing the verdict. When mere consultation with a lawyer could cost you an arm and a leg, here was this senior lawyer who hadn't charged me a single penny except for the court fee

In my naiveté, I didn't know that my court journey wasn't over yet, for what we had got was an ex parte injunction. What followed were some not so pleasant phone calls warning me that the court order would be turned around. Sure enough, the absent party this time decided to make an appearance to challenge the earlier court order and seek a reversal.

Mr Anand stood steadfast around me, telling me that this time they would need to prepare a lot more to be able to win the case. It is worthwhile to mention that this was one of the early cases in IP in the dot-com space and there was very little precedence available. 'I think we will need to reach out to another senior lawyer. I would suggest we get V.P. Singh on board,' Mr Anand's sentence put me in a tizzy. Here I was, not having paid Mr Anand a penny for his efforts, and certainly not in any position to afford the fee of another senior lawyer. Once again, Mr Anand came to my rescue and agreed to make a personal request to Mr Singh. True to his word, he did so and Mr Singh charged only some Rs 20,000-odd to represent me, as opposed to the lakhs he would otherwise charge for a personal appearance.

29 January 2002

Manish Vij and Ors. vs Indra Chugh and Ors.

No sooner was our case called out, than Mr V.P. Singh began his thundering representation. To start with, he made a mention of the fact that the word 'KabadiBazaar' was unique and was coined by us and that it did not appear in the dictionary, entitling us to its use to the exclusion of all others. He also argued that the domain name had achieved a great reputation on account of numerous articles written about it in newspapers and magazines as well as its coverage on TV. He then went on to point out that the defendants seemed to be in the habit of booking several domain names with which they had no connection and also that none of those websites were operational.

All the arguments bore fruit when their application was dismissed by the honourable court.

Among other things, the incident really reinforced my faith in the goodness of people and in serendipity. I realized that when you start off on a journey with the right intentions and without being paralysed with the worry of how you would overcome the obstacles on the way, a safety net appears. I was truly indebted to Mr Anand and his team for standing up for me. Incidentally, a few years after this event, once I had a stable job and had the financial capacity to make the payment that was rightfully due to him, I did reach out to him, only for him to laugh the matter away!

While high drama transpired in the court room on the issue of domain names, the story will be incomplete if I didn't tell you one more anecdote. At an entrepreneurial event post the case, I happened to meet a young boy, about the same age as me. 'Are you Manish Vij of KabadiBazaar?' he asked me out of nowhere. On my answering in the affirmative, he introduced himself as Ankush Johar. We generally got talking and the conversation veered towards the fact that I didn't own the surrounding domain names. I was pleasantly surprised to receive a call from Ankush the next day. What he had to say once again reaffirmed my faith in the goodness of people. 'I have booked and secured all the available extensions of KabadiBazaar (and similarly sounding names) for you at my own cost. You can take them for me any day', he said nonchalantly.

Mission Placement

While all of this went on to prove the amazing role that serendipity plays in life, what still remained to be seen was the impact of these efforts on my most important key responsibility area (KRA), namely, placements. Campus interviews were just beginning at the time and the first company to make an appearance on our campus was the digital division of the telecom behemoth, Bharti. There I was, ready to be interviewed by their General Manager (GM) Vikas Verma, alongside the top students in my college. A few minutes into the interview, and I knew that the intense planning and hard work to make my resumé stand out had indeed worked. Clearly all the hype around KabadiBazaar, and my practical experience had done the trick. I became the first person to be placed out of my entire batch. Offered a princely salary of Rs 11,000, I was placed with one of their divisions, MantraOnline in New Delhi. Mission placement had been accomplished and how!

The next few months went by quickly. I would spend the day at the Mantra Online office and the evenings working on *KabadiBazaar,* updating the many responses that the site was now flooded with. Besides the traffic and traction that the site was receiving, there was yet another curious validation of my business idea that I received once I joined Mantra Online. It turned out that the GM who had interviewed me had since then left the organization to work on launching a start-up. When I enquired further, I got to know that his start-up was, lo and behold, a somewhat similar website called KhulJaSimSim!

Top Ten Websites in India

I was blissfully unaware that the media coverage that had so far been my formula for KabadiBazaar's advertising success would soon turn into my nemesis. It so happened that *Business Today* carried a story featuring the top websites in the country and. KabadiBazaar was one of them. What complicated issues, however, was the fact that my employer, Mantra Online, was also on the list. I was really nervous at the thought of going in to work the next morning, not knowing how they would react. No sooner had I reached my desk than the intercom started to ring ominously. 'Mr N. Arjun (Mantra Online's CEO and my super boss) would like to see you right now,' my manager Anoop Mandal's voice left me in fear. In my mind, I was already seeing all the efforts I had made, being completely wasted. Who would have ever thought that the same media coverage that had brought me so far would now lead to my downfall? 'Manish, *tu toh gaya* (Manish, you are dead)!' was the pronouncement that my mind kept playing on loop.

No sooner had I entered N. Arjun's office than I began to apologize to him profusely. 'I promise to shut the website down, sir. I had launched it only so I could get a job. Do not fire me,' I went on and on, nearly incoherent. 'You will resign today,

Manish,' his words seemed to confirm my worst fears. What he said next wasn't something I was expecting to hear. 'You have a winner on your hands. You do not realize it. I want you to explore the full potential of this website. You will go far.' While his words were a balm for my pounding heart, I was at the same time extremely sceptical. When he heard the whole story of how I had launched the company with only Rs 75,000, he was even more surprised. 'I will connect you to potential investors. You must raise funds. Such opportunities do not come by easily.' While a part of me was happy to hear what he was saying, the fact that it needed me to quit my job, one that I had worked for, was heartbreaking. That evening as I headed home, I felt really dejected, not knowing what I would say to my parents. My fears, however, were unfounded as my parents were very supportive. 'If your super boss thinks you should start out on your own, there must be merit. Have faith in your capabilities,' my father said to me once I had narrated the events of the day. Looking back, the confidence of my parents was a recurring theme of my life. 'Manish, *dekhna kuch bada karega* (Manish, you will achieve something great),' was something I had heard my mother and grandmother say a million times throughout my childhood. This despite the fact that I was an average student. Their confidence and blessings, however, belied my academic abilities.

Armed with their blessings, I set out on an untravelled road. The next three to four months changed the trajectory of my life. Suddenly, from being a corporate executive who had just stepped on the first rung of the corporate ladder, I was thrown into the high world of VC funding. I found myself presenting business plans and making presentations, something I had never done before. One such meeting with Mr Abhay Havaldar, a reputed name in investment circles, saw me carrying six A4-sized printouts bound together with cello tape since I didn't know any better at the time.

Besides N. Arjun who led me to some of his VC contacts, some other leads that I received were from Ajit Balakrishnan, the founder of Rediff.com, one of the earliest Indian web portals, and its COO, Nitin Gupta. Rediff had contacted me initially wanting me to advertise kabadibazaar.com on their platform. They subsequently went out of their way to put me in touch with investors. I was on cloud nine on witnessing how, once I decided to take the leap, help had begun to appear from many unexpected directions.

This was a time when the US particularly was seeing a period of high market growth, coupled with the rapid growth of valuations in new dot-com start-ups. Its impact was beginning to trickle down to India. The future of the World Wide Web (WWW) was believed to hold tremendous potential as it promised to make everything faster, more efficient and more productive. Billions of dollars were flowing into start-ups, as each of them promised to use the Internet to change how humans shopped, worked, travelled and more. In anticipation, between 1995 and 2000, investments on the NASDAQ composite stock market index rose by a whopping 800 per cent. It seemed as if the party would never end. Only this was not the case.

It was when I was returning to Delhi after a particularly encouraging meeting with a large venture capital firm that had expressed an interest to invest in KabadiBazaar, that my world turned upside down. By the time the plane had touched the tarmac, news about the dot-com crash in the US had brought everything to a screeching halt. I quickly realized that the expression of interest that I held in my hand may not even be worth the piece of paper it was printed on anymore.

Within a few months, my world had crashed. I had lost my job while chasing a dream and now the dream had died too. 'Manish, *kya kar baitha tu* (How did you ruin it all)'? was all I could ask myself.

Actionable Insights

Start early: While it is never too late to find your purpose in life, the sooner you start the better it is. Typically, the twenties and early thirties are the best time to take bold bets. At the risk of generalising, as time goes by, you tend to be weighed down by life's responsibilities, witness a decline in energy and experience the baggage of limiting beliefs. It therefore works well to amass as much exposure, take as many risks as you can in the early years when your stakes aren't very high. This holds true not just in the context of entrepreneurship but also in other aspects of your career.

By starting early, you also attract the **power of compounding** that works in most aspects of life, be it the goal of financially retiring at 40, or areas such as relationships, knowledge, health, etc. I find the example of wanting to run the half marathon quite telling. In preparing for it, if you run the first 100 metres and incrementally add 100 metres every day to the previous day's run, you will soon be covering 21 kms, like a breeze.

Relationships run the world: Ever so often, we underestimate the value of our network. Many of us even believe that networking is a rather unpleasant task that involves trading favours with strangers. Done right, however, networking is far from exploitative, and inauthentic. It is about building genuine connections. All you have to do is to approach networking with a genuine heart and true interest in helping other people without personal interest. As the author Zig Ziglar says, 'You can have everything in life that you want, if you will just help other people get what they want.' Curiosity, empathy and most importantly, sincerity are ways to build long and trustworthy relationships. Truly, the real net worth of people can be measured not just in terms of their financial assets but in terms of trust-based relationship assets.

Chapter 4

Escape Velocity

'Happy Diwali!'

It was this seemingly innocuous greeting that turned my fortunes around.

By now, I had spent several weeks in a particularly dark state of mind. I was finding it hard to reconcile with the fact that I had come so close to raising funds for KabadiBazaar, before the dot-com crash had claimed my dreams. To keep going, I had picked up a job with a small website development company called Web Pulse that ran operations out of Greater Kailash 1 in Delhi. I was immediately able to build a warm rapport with the founder and senior team members, but my heart was clearly not in my work.

It was at this dark time in my life that Diwali, the festival of lights, brought with it a beacon of hope. It so happened that, in a conscious effort not to give in to the darkness within, I bought a number of Diwali cards (these were pre-WhatsApp times!) and sat down to send greetings to several people on my contact list. The list featured several names that I had interacted with during the peak of KabadiBazaar. One of the names that sprang out was that of Nitin Gupta, the COO of Rediff.com, who had been very helpful to me. The Diwali card to Nitin sent, I promptly forgot about it, until I was met with a return greeting from him. His personalized letter, acknowledging my Diwali wishes, ended with a customary line asking me to drop by at his office whenever I was in Mumbai. I decided to take Nitin up on his offer. While there was nothing that would take me to Mumbai anytime soon, I decided to do the next best thing—to make a call to him. It was during the course of our conversation that he asked me if I would be open to explore an opportunity to work as a strategist in Rediff's Delhi office. He ended our call with an encouraging 'You can meet Binod Chaudhary in Delhi and see if there is a mutual fit.'

I was ecstatic about the development and couldn't thank my stars enough for having sent those Diwali wishes. His last sentence, the suggestion that I should meet Binod, however, was a big dampener. Binod Choudhary and Vinay Mathews had first approached me from Rediff, wanting me to advertise my start-up KabadiBazaar on their platform. What complicated matters, was the fact that while I had no funding at the time, in my entrepreneurial zeal, I had discussed an advertising proposal for $200,000 (no less!) with Rediff.com. That too would have been fine had I then not gone on to question them about the efficacy of that proposal and to pull them up on a job badly done. While I was sceptical about the merits of approaching Binod, fortunately for me, he did not hold our last conversation against me. On the contrary, when I met him, he was quite receptive and I soon had a job with Rediff.com.

The next three years that I spent with Rediff were filled with great learning. I worked with Binod, who turned out to be a hard taskmaster as a boss. 'You can chew gum and cross the road,' he would say. His advice on multi-disciplinary learning stood me in good stead. Besides handling strategy and sales, I also got involved in several new projects such as the launch of Rediff Mobile, Rediff Mail and many others. In the process, not only was my own learning enhanced, I also became one of their leading performers. I was also lucky to be able to work with the COO, Nitin Gupta and the founder, Ajit Balakrishnan, quite closely. Importantly, Rediff also gave me an opportunity to interact with some of the best entrepreneurs on the other side, as clients. My years at Rediff saw me make some bold pitches to the founders of then young digital companies such as MakeMyTrip, Monster, Naukri, Shaadi, etc., leading to a huge increase in my networking and business skills.

Despite doing well in my job, scarred as I was by KabadiBazaar's untimely closure, I had decided that I should always have a Plan B in place. I therefore continued the yarn trading while also enrolling for coaching classes to prepare for the GMAT exam.

Turnaround

Come 2003, however, I could clearly see signs of a dotcom turnaround. Not only were advertising budgets on the Internet witnessing an upswing, we were also seeing a lot of activity from venture-funded Internet companies. Once again, I found myself feeling restless and itching to ride the entrepreneurial bandwagon. An idea that struck me at the time was to launch a digital advertising agency since I noticed first-hand how traditional advertising agencies didn't quite understand this new medium. The digital advertising space was a relatively virgin territory with only two such agencies in operation—the then Martin Sorrell-led WPP's GroupM and MediaTurf, set up by advertising veteran V. Ramani. A basic analysis done, I convinced my immediate boss at Rediff, Aditya Verma, to be a part of this proposed venture. Aditya and I would often sit at his home after office hours, putting together elaborate business plans.

Before I took the final leap though, I wanted to run our business plan through an expert in the field. This led me to my dear friend Sanchit Sanga, who worked at GroupM at the time, the largest in the business. 'Can you have a look at this business plan? *Isme profit nahi dikh raha* (I can't see any profit here). Is it worth pursuing?' I quizzed him. After taking a close look at the Excel sheet, Sanchit shut my laptop with a firm hand and turned towards me. 'Manish, you have to start somewhere. At this stage, I cannot tell you where the profits will come from, but they will follow. Just start,' he said, with a sense of finality.

While I was greatly encouraged by Sanchit's words, subconsciously I hadn't fully recovered from KabadiBazaar's unfortunate closure and wanted to be doubly sure. Therefore,

I decided that prior to starting out, I should have an actual client in my fold. The desire to have a revenue-first business plan led Aditya and me to approach Arun Tadanki, a very dear friend and the then country manager at Monster.com. They had recently acquired JobsAhead.com and were advertising heavily. Little did we know at the time that the meeting would turn things on its head.

'What you have is a margin-diminishing business model. Personally, I wouldn't recommend that you pursue the ad agency idea,' Arun said, on hearing of our plan, throwing us into a tizzy.

'Instead, why don't the two of you join me at Monster?' came his counter-offer, something that we hadn't expected at all. As we shook hands, I tried my best to hide how disheartened I felt.

On my way out, I decided to stop by and meet Alok Mittal, the founder of JobsAhead.com—who sat in the same office building, as perhaps the acquisition handover was still taking place. The customary greetings offered, Alok asked me what had brought me to their office. Once I explained the purpose of the visit and its outcome, I ended my monologue by saying that I would now need to think of a new business idea. While Alok listened to me patiently, what he said to me was life-changing.

'There is something known as an escape velocity,' he said, referring to a concept of physics that speaks of a minimum speed that is required for an object to free itself from the gravitational force. 'Instead of worrying about what business model you will choose, try to reach that escape velocity that gets you into orbit in the first place. Once you are there, you will find many other ideas,' he said, with certainty.

Just hearing Alok say this shifted something in me internally. I realized that I had to make that first move and not be unduly bogged down by a vicious cycle of 'what ifs'. By the time I sat in the car, I was certain that I was ready to give my entrepreneurial dreams wings, once again!

There was yet another surprise waiting for me. When my eyes met Aditya's in the car, his eyes seemed to be lit up too. Encouraged, I blurted out, '*Main soch raha hoon, start kar doon* (I am thinking of starting out),' only to hear Aditya saying, as if on cue, '*Main soch raha hoon, Monster join kar loon* (I am thinking of joining Monster).'

Clearly it was time for us to part ways and get into different orbits.

Actionable Insights

Find your escape velocity: Uncertainty cannot be wished away or fully countered through detailed business plans. In my experience, the only way to actually find your escape velocity is by getting into the entrepreneurial trenches and getting your hands dirty. Pick a problem that matters and that aligns with the purpose that drives you. It helps if the industry you have chosen is young, with high potential and has many open opportunities that are ready to embrace disruption. Twenty-five years ago, I chose the Internet-led tech industry and found my calling. That said, do not wait for your higher purpose to dawn on you. Remember, a good plan today is better than a perfect plan tomorrow.

In choosing entrepreneurship, however, be prepared to embrace a life that is hugely uncertain, hard and lonely. If your reasons for turning to entrepreneurship aren't strong enough, you are likely to fall out along the way. On the other hand, if your reasons are strong enough, the universe as they say, will conspire to help you reach your goals. Remember though to cut the noise and surround yourself with believers who will help you bring your A-game to the table.

Be open to feedback: A person's innate nature is often inherent and remains relatively consistent throughout life, but personality is something that can and should evolve with effort. Improving personality is a lifelong process, requiring a willingness to seek, observe and act on constructive feedback from all sources. While many tend to regard feedback as criticism, taken in the right spirit, it is a valuable opportunity for self-reflection. The ability to seek and act upon constructive feedback, in fact, has been life changing in my journey. In many situations, perception is bigger than reality, and this insight has personally driven me to work on improving several habits while recognizing that I still have many areas for improvement. I have benefited from several people who have become life-coaches of sorts, in helping me identify and address my blind spots. It is my firm belief that having the capability to listen feedback is a powerful tool for entrepreneurs that can drive both personal and professional growth.

Chapter 5

The Power of Saying No

No co-founder and no client.

That was the spot I found myself in after my meeting at Monster.com. Admittedly it wasn't the best place for a wannabe founder, except that I was now determined to find my escape velocity.

At this time a meeting with a dear friend, Sachin Bhatia, co-founder at MakeMyTrip, turned out to be a gamechanger. Sachin introduced me to Harish Bahl, who ran a company called Studio Smile, one of the tech partners for MakeMyTrip. An outgoing Punjabi, in equal parts sharp and warm, Harish and I got along fairly quickly. An engineer by education, Harish had begun his career building bulletproof cars in his father's workshop. He later started Studio Smile, with his college mate and co-founder C.P. Singh, taking up web development work. Harish and C.P. had gone on to build the business from a one-room office in Lajpat Nagar to an approximately thirty-people web and tech development business in Delhi's Zamrudpur.

I was not only discussing business ideas with Harish, the two of us were also looking at shifting homes at the time. While my family was looking at moving out from Triveni Apartments in Paschim Vihar in West Delhi to South Delhi, Harish's family was looking to move from their home in Delhi's Lajpat Nagar. Shared house-hunting goals led us to meet often. It was these continued meetings that led us to the idea of starting a 'digital creative services business process outsourcing (BPO)' business together. We briefly began operations by placing one person in the Studio Smile office. While this business shut down quickly because we received more demand than we were set up to deliver, Harish's warm nature, his boldness towards work and the fact that we gelled well together helped me come to a decision to partner with him.

While Harish and I decided to start a new digital media agency together, it was agreed that I would continue to work at Rediff until the new company could afford to pay the salary of the first couple of team members. We also agreed that Harish's partner in Studio Smile, C.P. Singh, who was a tech wizard, would come in as our third co-founder. Sceptical of partnerships in general, I felt that we should at the outset, agree on how we would resolve disagreements, should we have any. Since Harish was six years my senior and came with considerable experience in the business space, I immediately conceded that it was his word that would prevail in times of a conflict, a commitment that I have kept to, ever since.

The Birth of Quasar

The search for a name for our company once again led us to Sachin Bhatia, a marketing whiz and co-founder of MakeMyTrip. One of the names that he suggested was Quasar, which meant the brightest star in the galaxy. What attracted us to the name was its international feel, ambitious as we were to one day make a mark globally!

We had the luxury to start operations from the Studio Smile office; what we needed now was a team to run operations and, importantly, a client to get us to hit that opening run. While I had drawn out a list of clients that we could approach—clients that I had known and worked with—none were ready to sign on the dotted line just yet.

'Come To Paris'

The subject line of an email that hit our mailbox one day caught our attention. While we were desperately looking for domestic clients, we had also written to a large international company, Real Media, which served most banners on the Internet in those days. It was in response to our mail, suggesting that they should explore the sizable Indian market, that they had invited us to Paris to have a meeting with them. We were in a fix. On the one hand, we were excited at a potential opportunity, but the fact that we would need to spend money to travel to Paris for a meeting, without knowing what was in store for us, sounded too risky. Harish and I, however, decided to bite the bullet. We set out on a frugal backpacking trip, digging into our savings. Landing in Paris, we were invited to the meeting that was to be held at a fancy sushi restaurant, a concept that was alien to us at the time. Our only exposure to 'foreign' food in those days was Chinese fare, and even that came in its Indianized avatar. The fact that I was a vegetarian was a godsend as I could make do with some soup, while I responded to their queries about the potential of India as a market. Harish, however, had a difficult task cut out for him. Not only did he have to swallow sashimi (sliced raw fish), he also had to make appreciative remarks about its taste. The meeting concluded. we stepped out only to find Harish puking. We knew that we had to look for an Indian restaurant in the vicinity to satiate our desi palate.

Back in Delhi, we had an excruciating wait to see if the meeting would indeed fructify. There was, however, another curious repercussion that my Paris trip led to. My parents, worried that this could be the beginning of my solo trips abroad, decided that it was time to get me married and have me 'settled'. Through an arranged marriage set-up, I was introduced to Tina, who is now my wife. Hailing from Mandi Dabwali in Haryana, her family and ours knew each other through a dear family friend, Rishabh Raizada. I first met Tina at Hotel Grand at Vasant Kunj. Occupied as I was with my business plans, all I could offer by way of conversation was a prosaic 'Do you want to share anything about yourself and your family with me?' Of the fifteen-minute conversation that followed, Tina spoke for nearly twelve. At the end of the meeting with her, a mutual confidence in each other's family made us say 'Yes'. That and the fact that I had heard Ashok chacha, my local guardian while I was at college in Indore, say that for any marriage to be successful, compatibility had to be built over time. There was something about Tina that gave me the confidence that we could build that compatibility. It turned out that the confidence was well placed since Tina and I have spent over twenty years together. Not only has Tina stood with me through thick and thin, she has also been a very strong motivator and a pillar of strength and confidence.

In hindsight, Tina is also the one who brought me some much-needed luck. When I met her for the customary first meeting, I was an employee at Rediff; by our second date, however, the tide had turned and I was ready to take on the world of entrepreneurship with Quasar. I recall how at our second date at Cafe Coffee Day at Safdarjung Enclave in Delhi, I pulled out a tissue to explain my entrepreneurial plans to her. That it had Tina's concurrence was a source of great confidence for me.

Sight of the First Client

'*Monster se meeting mil gayi hai, bechana kya hai* (We have a meeting with Monster. What do you want me to sell to them)?' Harish's excitement and nervousness were both palpable on the phone call he made to me one morning just as I entered the Rediff office. On my request, Arun Tadanki of Monster and his Marketing Head, Gayatri, had agreed to explore business opportunities with us. Only since I was still a Rediff employee, this meeting would have to be helmed by Harish, who didn't know much about the technicalities of the digital media business. 'You need to tell them that beyond Rediff, we will also offer them a bouquet of publishers to drive their traffic through digital media,' was my brief to Harish as he set out for the meeting with Gopikaa, a colleague. Harish's next phone call to me in a couple of hours, as I boarded a DTC bus to head home, was jubilant. 'We got the business,' he exclaimed. 'I just kept repeating the phrase you had taught me—bouquet of publishers,' he said, breaking out into laughter.

With a major client in our kitty in keeping with our revenue-first approach, our next step now was to have a team member on board. I approached Deven, my best friend, whose father and mine had been college mates. Deven had always been my partner in crime. At this time, he was working at Andhra Paper Mill and wasn't too happy with its traditional set-up. I remember reaching out to his mother to convince him to take my offer. I promised that he would soon earn a five-digit salary, even though I myself didn't quite know how. Having convinced Deven, the next step was to get Harish to interview him. I still recall the call from Harish after he had conducted Deven's interview to say he doesn't know anything about digital media, to which I retorted with '*Sab aa jaayega* (he will learn everything).' The strategy worked and Quasar Media had its first official employee on board.

Soon I was ready to say goodbye to my corporate career and to wear the hat of an entrepreneur. I distinctly recall the last deal that I closed at Rediff just before moving on. A hard negotiation with Sanjeev Bikhchandani and Hitesh Oberoi of Naukri.com resulted in one of the largest deals during my stint at Rediff. The deal closed, I met up with Sanjeev a couple of weeks later and informed him of my decision to start a digital media advertising company. Armed with Sanjeev's good wishes, I felt that much more comfortable in beginning my new journey. Given my rapport with Sanjeev, I knew that he was one person I could reach out to for advice in my entrepreneurial career as well.

The one important thing left to do now was to meet Ajit Balakrishnan, the founder of Rediff.com, where my career had found a new lease of life after my first entrepreneurial venture had failed to take off. 'The doors of Rediff are always open for you,' his gracious remark, once he sensed that I was ready to take flight, filled me with enthusiasm.

The big milestones in my personal and professional life were colliding as my foray into entrepreneurship was timed with my wedding with Tina. I was so caught up with everything happening at the professional front that I had decided to give my honeymoon a miss. It was the advice of Charles Jenarius, the then Head of Carat Media, a global media and marketing agency, that made me change my mind. 'You will enjoy a number of holidays with your wife but never a honeymoon. Do not miss this opportunity,' he had told me. It was on his advice that Tina and I headed out on our honeymoon to Australia, spending almost everything that I had saved so far.

It was while I was on my honeymoon in Australia that I received a call from Sandeep Singh, a young team member at Rediff. 'Sir, I have resigned,' he said, over the crackle of a long-distance call. 'Where are you joining?' I asked. 'I am joining you, of course,' he said, to my surprise. '*Abhi toh meri hi salary ka kuch pata nahi* (Right now, I have no idea how to pay myself). How will we afford your salary?' I asked. '*Dekhi jayegi* (We will see),' was his confident response. There you go, the second team member at Quasar had literally invited himself over. Sandeep would go on to play a strong role in Quasar's growth.

Sandeep's confidence wasn't misplaced, for we soon went on to acquire our second client. If our first client brought us joy, the second client sent me on a short trip down memory lane. For this client was Airtel, a part of Bharti Enterprises, the company that also owned Mantra Online, where I had started my corporate career and that had led me on to my eventful, albeit short-lived journey with KabadiBazaar. Prashant Tandon at Airtel trusted us with his digital media campaign that was designed to generate customer leads for Airtel broadband. It was the first digital campaign at Airtel that was released through Quasar, bypassing Airtel's long-standing advertising agency, Madison Media.

Strategic Offers

While we were beginning to acquire clients, surprisingly what we were also beginning to receive were buyout offers early on in our journey. The Internet at the time was like a blue ocean and there were very few digital media agencies that understood the medium, leading many to be interested in our offerings. The first of these intentions came from Charles Jenarius, who I had met in the course of pitching for business. Charles had made it clear that, his company Carat Media—a part of Aegis—a global media giant, wanted to explore a strategic opportunity with us. While that conversation was on, we received a surprise guest in our office. Sam Balsara was a doyen of Indian media and an extremely well-respected name in media circles. He was the founder of Madison Media, the agency that handled the Airtel account. Understandably so, he was upset that Airtel had decided to release a portion of their campaign, admittedly small, through Quasar. Cutting straight to the chase, he made us an offer, wanting to buy our agency out. The offer, however, wasn't too lucrative from our standpoint. 'Sam, would you be open for negotiations?' Harish asked him point-blank. 'When I make an offer, I do not go back and forth,' came Mr Balsara's immediate response. Not aware of the towering figure that Sam Balsara cut in the industry, Harish countered it with '*Agar aap apni industry ke Sam hain, toh Manish bhi apni industry ka Sam hai* (If you are the Sam of your industry, Manish is also well renowned in his industry),' much to my embarrassment, as Sam continues to be a person I hold in high regard.

While the buyout did not take place, what really did take off was Quasar's growth. The fact that Studio Smile, Harish and CP's company, was already running as a technology and creative services firm, helped in fast tracking Quasar's success. We did not have to deal with teething troubles that start-ups commonly face. Instead, we could focus our energies on acquiring new clients. Importantly, Quasar built a strong reputation for offering transparent and performance-led digital media plans and was recognized by industry folks as the first to do so.

Not only did we have large clients in our kitty, encouragingly we were also beginning to see profits. Prior to beginning our operations, I had chalked out a list of ten probable clients with whom I had existing relationships, hoping that they would help me kick-start the business. As it turned out, growth at Quasar in those early months came from a whole new set of clients that I could not have even anticipated.

It was about time I took a deep breath and reminded myself about the advice given by Sanchit Sanga and Alok Mittal in the early stages of setting up Quasar. It was these two gentlemen who had convinced me not to overthink and to find my escape velocity, and that clients and profits would follow.

When it Rains, it Pours

It was during my early days at Rediff, that I had first heard that there was this large technology company called Google that was making its presence felt in the US. This company, I learnt, was focusing on online advertising and had started giving out advertising contracts to publishers. I had decided at the time to take an audacious leap of faith and send a ten-slide presentation to them, telling them exactly why they needed to set up operations in India. The presentation was sent as a cold email to an address I had found on the Internet, that of David Lee, a member of Google's New Business Development Team. While I sent the email and forgot about it, in a couple of days, I received a reply from Lee. It stated that his colleague, Vikram Grover, was visiting India and that I should meet him. Subsequent to that preliminary meeting, there were other sporadic meetings and phone calls with Google every few months. Nothing concrete, however, had taken shape. While my interest in these meetings was to build advertising revenue for Rediff, Google was interested in evaluating my ability to build a market for them in India.

This time, however, two years after I had dropped that first email to Google and while I was a few months into setting up Quasar, came yet another email. This one was from Sukhinder Singh Cassidy, General Manager at Google and a big name in

Silicon Valley. It said that they were keen to start operations in India and that they had decided to roll out an offer to me for which I needed to visit Mumbai. A bit in a trance and not too sure what would come out of the meeting, I decided to go along and make a trip to Mumbai anyway. What followed was an actual offer letter, one that offered me the post of Sales Manager for India—one of the two positions they were finalizing for the India business. I was offered a huge salary along with Restricted Stock Units. 'Google is the fastest growing company in the world. *Iss salary mein toh hum Ford Endeavour bhi le sakte hain* (We can buy a Ford Endeavour with this salary),' I remember telling Tina, my desire for a fancy car raising its head. My enthusiasm was met with a calm 'Think it through' from her.

After my initial euphoria subsided came the realization that having begun Quasar, I now carried the responsibility of my team members. Other than Deven and Sandeep, by this time, we had also inducted a gentleman named Hitesh Dhingra, who was Sandeep's college mate and had come from Singapore on glowing recommendation from Sandeep. Clearly, I couldn't leave my team in the lurch. On raising the issue with Google, they assured me that while the recruitments would have to follow the formal recruitment process at Google, they were open to the idea. It was only five months since Quasar had begun operations and while business was coming in, there was still a bit of nervousness about the future. That further tilted the scale in Google's favour and I found myself dreaming of working for one of the world's best companies in the digital sector as a part of their leadership team with a very fat salary, stock options and, of course, a fancy car.

Harish was visiting Australia at the time and the only task I was left with was to break the news to him and convince him that it was too good an offer for me to let go. I had, however, underestimated the task of convincing him. On breaking the news to him, he asked me if I had sought my dad's opinion on it. I had shared the news with my father, of course, and while my father had agreed that the offer was great, he, much like Tina, had asked me to calmly think of all the pros and cons before coming to any decision.

Before I knew it, Harish had cut short his Australia trip and landed up at my father's office. '*Ladke ka dimaag kharab ho gaya hai* (the boy has lost his mind),' Harish told my dad, asking him to convince me not to take up the offer. Subsequent to meeting Harish, my dad called me, asking me to come and see him at his office. What he had to say now wasn't very different from what he had said last time, except that he wanted me to think through the fact that not everyone gets an opportunity to start up. 'Getting a prestigious job such as this is hard but starting a business that's showing signs of success is harder,' he said, perhaps referring to his own experience especially since he had harboured the desire to set up a spinning yarn business. 'If tomorrow your business does not do well, you will still have an opportunity to find another job. To be able to build the same momentum for a start-up one more time, however, may not be that easy. Age is also on your side. Think about it,' he said, leaving the final decision, as always, to me. Something about the way my dad spoke shifted something within me. The conversation made me realize that the journey of life would always come with its temptations; it is the ability to stick to your goal that will eventually lead you to success.

Armed with this new-found understanding, I reached out to Google to tell them that, grateful as I was for their offer, I couldn't accept it. While they were willing to relook at the offer, I politely turned the offer down, confessing to them that I had already found the salary very attractive and the only reason I was saying no was to focus on my company. This was a decision that turned out well for me, in hindsight.

It was a couple of years later that I met Sukhinder at an airport along with their then Country Manager, Shailesh Rao. 'Hey, Manish! I hear it is going well for you guys. By the way, any regrets about not joining Google?' Sukhinder asked me, only to be met with an instant 'No' from my side. 'Why?' she asked, a bit taken aback with my immediate response. 'Because now even I can hire someone like Shailesh,' I responded intuitively, not with any hubris, armed instead with a far clearer vision.

This is an incident that Shailesh and I share a good laugh about even now, each time we happen to meet, both of us having struck up a friendship.

Actionable Insights

Irrational self-belief: Having zeroed in on an idea, what is most needed is a kind of self-belief that may seem to border on the irrational, to see you through. You need to believe that you can recruit better than others, make the best product decisions and that you and your team will go that extra mile to make everything possible.

Asking for help is a power move: Much as we may want to be in command of every situation, neither our business plans nor life tends to stay true to the way we plan it. In such situations, you need to make use of what is probably the hardest four-letter word to utter in business or in life: HELP. More so, since we have been conditioned to think that we are 'less than' if we ask for help from others. I was therefore extremely taken in when I read this quote by the author and professor Brene Brown, 'Asking for help is a power move. It's a sign of strength to ask and a sign of strength to fight off judgement when other people raise their hands'. Truly when we find the courage to ask for help, we aren't just being strong ourselves, we are also creating a ripple effect and giving others the permission to do the same. Looking back, not being afraid of showing my vulnerability, reaching out to people and seeking help has always come to my aid.

The attitude of gratitude: It is my firm belief that in good times and bad, gratitude raises your vibration and signals to the universe that you are receptive to its guidance. It shifts your focus from lack to abundance, helping you attract more of what you need. Remember, gratitude is like a muscle, the more time you spend building it, the bigger it grows.

Chapter 6

There Are No Rules

GroupM

Very early when we were still a small team, those were the six letters that were printed in a large font and pasted on the exit door of our office. It was a standard ritual for all of us to look at that poster each time we walked out of the door. Anybody visiting our office would have been shocked at this largish display of our competitor's name in our office, on the exit door, no less. Except that the insanity wasn't misplaced. If anything, it was targeted well. GroupM was a leading global advertising agency that we respected, one that we recognized as our 'Enemy Number 1' and were determined to beat. A reminder to do so every day kept each of us focused on a common goal.

Come to think of it, ours was a small team with large aspirations. We had a standing joke at Quasar as we travelled for meetings in the old Scorpio that C.P. Singh, owned. '*Poori company ek Scorpio mein aa jati hai* (The whole company fits into a Scorpio),' we would quip. The fact was that, in those early days, we were more than a company. The founding team and the first few team members were family to each other. We had a strong bond, one that founder's equity or ESOPs or any amount of monetary compensation could not replicate. It was because the bond was driven by a common passion for making an impact that we created many firsts in the industry and received widespread recognition in the ecosystem. The business was growing profitably, and we had 30 per cent market share of our industry within the first three years of starting up.

For our part as founders, we made sure that the founding team members could equally bask in this glory. Each time, for instance, that Quasar was covered in the media for a new client acquisition or for delivering a great campaign, we made sure that the contribution of the team member in charge of the account was acknowledged. I had anticipated that these accolades would keep the team morale high. What I couldn't have ever imagined is that it would also help them in their personal life (read matrimonial pursuits). Yet that's exactly how it turned out to be. It so happened that I once got a call for a reference check for Sandeep Singh, a founding team member of Quasar. The caller, Sandeep's prospective father-in-law, wanted to know how the 'boy' was doing. Since start-ups were considered far from fashionable at that time, I could appreciate that this gentleman wanted some endorsement of the potential groom. All I had to do was tell him to Google 'Sandeep Singh'. Sure enough, a quick Google search threw up a lot of media coverage that mentioned both Quasar and Sandeep and laid the gentleman's doubts to rest. That wedding bells followed soon, is a given!

A Term Sheet

Charles Jenarius, who had shown a desire to enter into a strategic relationship with us early on, directed us to his holding company, Aegis Media, at this time. Among other people, we were led to meet the chief digital officer at Aegis, a gentleman called Nigel Morris who was considered a big name in the digital advertising world in the US. With Nigel slated to visit us at our Zamrudpur office, we were trying to make sure that his visit went smoothly. On the appointed day, however, the street had a fresh blow of cow dung. As if that wasn't enough by way of welcome, someone decided to spit paan, missing Nigel narrowly, as he got out of his car. That initial embarrassment apart, the meeting was a breeze. We were absolutely blown away by Nigel's storytelling skills as well as some of the insights that he brought to the table. So potent was our desire to learn and imbibe the cutting-edge work happening in the industry globally that we promptly incorporated many of the learnings he shared with us into the Quasar deck.

While we were hard at work building our business, Aegis came back to us with an offer. They were keen to buy a majority stake in Quasar, while putting the balance on an earnout (a provision whereby the seller receives additional payments based on the future performance of the business sold). None of us founders had seen this kind of money before, having made our way up from humble backgrounds. We, therefore, decided to reach out to some industry veterans to seek their view. The first name that came to my mind was that of Ajit Balakrishnan, my super boss at Rediff.com, a very respected name in the field. 'If you had to sell your company, what would you do?' I asked him. 'I would either sell all 100 per cent or a minority stake,' he answered categorically. Back in office, Harish and I discussed his recommendation. It was perhaps the sheer size of the offer and the fact that we were relatively new and inexperienced in our journey that led us to decide that we could ignore Ajit's advice and agree to Aegis's offer and accept their term sheet. It was only in hindsight, in quite another context, that we realized how prudent Ajit's advice was, for selling a majority stake in your company is like having your own wings cut off and being reduced to working like an employee. But I digress.

While Aegis was quick to offer us a term sheet, they were quite slow with the subsequent processes. While the long-stop date mentioned in the term sheet soon flew by, they kept engaging with us, even calling us to San Francisco for a meeting.

While they took their own sweet time, we continued to work hard at expanding our portfolio and adding new clients to our kitty. Another important aspect that we undertook during this period was to strengthen our management team. We reached out to Mahender Swaroop, another industry veteran, who was the CEO of Indiatimes at the time and was due to retire. Not only did he agree to invest some capital, in the form of warrants, in our company, he also agreed to take on the role of a mentor. In a way, it was like getting the founder's boss in the interest of the company's growth, credibility and having a strong advisor on board.

Hasna Nahin Hai

One of the large accounts that we had acquired in those days was that of Microsoft. Besides being a prestigious client, it also had a dream client team of Anurag Gaur, Vineet Durrani and Ranjivjit Singh, who we loved working with. We did not leave any stone unturned in coming up with innovative ideas and trying to grow the Microsoft business in India. We also worked very closely with their agency, Wunderman Thompson, and with a gentleman called Pete Pierce, who had been deputed from France to handle the client in India. By this time, given Aegis's interest in us, word had spread in advertising circles that Quasar was open to a potential strategic offer. Pete broached the issue with us, asking us if we would be open to Wunderman looking at a potential buyout of Quasar. It was he who connected us to WPP, their holding company. Since Aegis's long-stop date was long over, we were well within our rights to explore other avenues. Armed with a glowing recommendation from Pete, we were called for a meeting with WPP's celebrity founder, Sir Martin Sorrell. In the advertising world, no one was a bigger celebrity than him, known as he was for going on a global acquisition spree to build the world's largest advertising company, WPP.

A closed-door conversation held at Maurya Sheraton in New Delhi was graced by Martin Sorrell with Harish, C.P. Singh and me in attendance. 'This is my co-founder, Manish; he heads the business side. This is my other co-founder, C.P. Singh who takes care of tech,' as the CEO of the company, Harish, began the proceedings by making the introductions. 'And do you serve coffee in the office?' came Sorrell's retort, a testament to his sharpness, since Harish had missed introducing himself. The comment had us all in peals of laughter. There couldn't have been a better icebreaker. The meeting proceeded very well from there. As the meeting drew to a close, Sorrell stated that he was keen on a strategic alliance and that his colleagues, Shay Amin and Mark Read, the current CEO of WPP, would be in touch with us to take the discussion forward.

The next thing we knew was that we were on a call with Shay Amin to negotiate the terms of the offer. In our minds, we knew that even though Aegis's long-stop date had gone by, they were still interested in us. Besides, we were growing a profitable company and had no pressing compulsion to sell out. Armed with this confidence, we decided to quote an amount that was higher than Aegis's offer. Not just that, we also decided to go a few steps further and tell Amin that we would not be willing to sign a term sheet and that if they were interested, they should be signing a Shareholders Agreement (SHA) with us straightaway, an unheard-of thing when it came to such deals. In our hearts, Harish and I didn't think that they would agree, but we decided to take an aggressive stance since there was nothing to lose anyway. For good measure, we also added that all of this should be done within a time frame of thirty days. In our minds, we were fully prepared that since we were being so audacious, the deal may not go through. To our surprise, perhaps even shock, we were not met with any resistance from the other side, with Amin ending the call with 'Give me a few days.'

The Hyatt Regency in New Delhi was the seat of our next meeting. By then, Mr Swaroop had joined us and we had requested him not just to accompany us for this important meeting but also to lead it. 'Mr Swaroop, let us not blink. You stick to the number. I don't think Harish or I can do it. We are sure to break into laughter if we put on a stern negotiating face and try to stick to this high figure,' I remember us telling him. In keeping with our strategy, Mr Swaroop helmed the meeting and stayed firm on the figure that we had quoted. As the meeting drew to a close, we couldn't really believe our ears when we heard the team from WPP say 'The deal is on.' Not only had WPP agreed to our figure, the standard rules of signing a term sheet prior to an SHA had also been flouted.

Under the table, Harish and I squeezed each other's hands to pulp, in an attempt to remind ourselves—*hasna nahin hai* (we shouldn't laugh).

What that deal taught us above anything else was that if you ran your business well and were not desperate to crack a deal, you could definitely surpass your highest expectations!

There was a small piece of the puzzle, however, that needed to be solved before we could sign the SHA. WPP wanted to acquire Quasar along with Studio Smile. While I was a shareholder at Quasar, Studio Smile was a company that Harish and C.P. had been running for a while. While they were okay with including Studio Smile in the deal, the task at hand was merging the equities of two companies, one in which I was a shareholder and the other in which I wasn't.

Harish, C.P. and I sat down for a late-night chat. 'Equities are never fair; this discussion can be over in a couple of minutes or it can take a lifetime. It depends upon how we handle it,' said Harish. For early-stage companies where a lot of build-up work is yet to be done, there were no benchmarks to go by. Also, you cannot say with certainty which of the companies will surpass the other, in terms of growth. We clearly had to come to an intuitive decision. I was reminded of the time when we had set up Quasar, and I had committed to Harish that in times of conflict, it was his decision that would prevail. It was time to honour that commitment. I left the decision of deciding the equity that I should hold in the combined venture, to Harish. He suggested a number and I agreed, thereby ending the discussion in five minutes.

Actionable Insights

Optimize for a common value system: In hiring team members, the traits that we typically look for are domain expertise, intelligence and go-getting ability. The one critical factor that we tend to miss is whether or not they share a 'common value system' with us—i.e., the cultural suitability. Very often, it is the misalignment in the value system that leads to inefficiency or even the breakdown of teams.

Some of the values that I have lived by and looked for are: Passion over pedigree, company first approach and ownership and integrity.

One hack that has come to my aid in this process is to optimize for 'referenced' hiring. In building core teams, I have relied on good friends, well known colleagues in previous companies, someone who comes with a strong reference from an industry contact etc. That way there are greater chances of a cultural fit. As the team grows in size, you also need to ensure that organizational values are documented, talked about with pride and spread through action by the founder and top leadership.

The founder's responsibility, of course, does not end here. Having found team members that have a good combination of domain expertise and the right value system, you then need to offer an environment where they can thrive. It is important to treat employees like family members and build emotional connections. In my entrepreneurial life I have always believed in a culture of common learning and growth as opposed to a hire and fire culture. In the end, team building is about finding high quality and culturally fit people, enabling and motivating them, supporting them in their growth and working on retaining them.

'What is your moat?' This is one of the most common questions that stakeholders ask. While moats continue to evolve—the one constant moat for any business is 'an emotionally engaged team with a shared value system'.

Chapter 7

The Power of a Dream

It was a momentous day, one that changed something for us irrevocably. The SHA for the Quasar deal was signed late evening in WPP's lawyers' office. The dotted line signed, WPP had officially acquired a majority stake in Quasar while putting the balance on an earnout. While setting up Quasar, some three-odd years ago, none of us could ever have dreamt of such a figure hitting our company's bank account anytime soon. I recall taking a screenshot of the amount and looking at it several times that evening to convince myself that I was indeed living this reality.

Before we could call it a day and go back to our families to celebrate, there was one important task that needed to be accomplished. The founding team of eight key people at Quasar needed to be acknowledged for this milestone! None of them had ever raised claims to a potential shareholding in the company but we knew that they had a huge role in getting us to this landmark. Back then, we didn't know the concept of ESOPs but in our minds, they were partners in building the company. A founding team that was more like a family.

'Can we meet on the terrace of the office at 10 p.m.?' read our message to the team. While each of them knew that the WPP deal was in the works, what they didn't know was what was in store for them that night. The announcement of the news of the SHA having been signed led to a huge round of applause that broke the silence of the night. What followed, however, left everyone stumped. 'While we have not rolled out our ESOPs, you all are rightful shareholders/partners of the company. All of you will be eligible to receive a part of the company exit, as rightful shareholders, as the company has achieved an important milestone,' we declared. For a while, the statement was met with absolute silence; it was as if they were all in a trance. Until someone started to clap—that broke the floodgates. The very air that night, as we stood on that terrace, seemed to be buzzing with pride and joy.

Deep Kalra, the founder of MakeMyTrip, had once said to me that the level of happiness that a founder feels when his team members can buy their first home from the earnings of the company, is unparalleled. While at that time, I couldn't appreciate the full import of his statement, today I could feel a sense of unadulterated joy. The money that each of them earned would go a long way in transforming their lives. On our part, as founders, we were grateful that God had made us an instrument to drive this change.

A few days later, the news of the Quasar sale having created several 'crorepatis' in the Internet industry would be all over the media—a first for its times back in 2008.

After signing up with WPP, we met Vikram Sakhuja, the then CEO of GroupM in India, for an introductory meeting. A lot of laughter flowed as we revealed how in building Quasar, we had focused on GroupM as our 'enemy number 1' and how that helped us to dream big.

Picture Abhi Baaki Hai

'Quasar enters into a JV with WPP'—that was the headline of the story that found place in several leading publications the next morning. Rightly so, as the Quasar–WPP deal was one of the largest acquisition deals done in the country at the time. It was to Harish's credit, that in making a formal announcement of the deal, he stated that Quasar had entered into a JV with WPP as opposed to saying that the company had been sold. Not only was he correct technically since we still held a minority shareholding in the company, importantly, it made all the difference in terms of the message that was being sent out. At that moment if we considered Quasar as having been sold to WPP, we would land up adopting an employee mindset. It was important that we kept our minds 'unlocked' even as we worked as a part of the WPP ecosystem.

Another important development that had taken place while we structured the deal with WPP, that enabled us to achieve this mental 'unlock', was that we had managed to keep a division of Quasar—Tyroo—outside the deal. Tyroo was an ad tech platform that we had launched only a few months ago. This was a time when Google had just about started building its own ad network. As I was driving to work one day, it was almost like an epiphany, as it struck me that if we built an ad network ourselves, it could give us a head start, especially as we could introduce it to Quasar's clients. The name, Tyroo, was suggested by Sandeep Singh as he felt that companies with 'double Os' in their names seemed to be weaving some magic—be it Google or Yahoo. We thus started Tyroo as a division within Quasar.

Just as the conversation with WPP for Quasar's acquisition was underway, Pearl Uppal, a dear friend and a former colleague at Rediff, who now worked as Senior Sales Leader at Yahoo India, reached out to me to say that Yahoo would be interested in exploring a strategic opportunity with Tyroo. We realized at the time that if Tyroo went away along with Quasar to WPP, we would stand to miss an opportunity. We therefore decided to speak to WPP to keep Tyroo outside the purview of the deal. It wasn't a tough thing to negotiate as WPP's mission was to acquire profitable companies alone. We pointed out to them that Tyroo was a tech division within the company that was to be run like a tech company, and not as a service organization. That made the decision for WPP and they agreed to let Tyroo remain outside the purview of the deal.

On our part, we went on to launch Smile Interactive Technology Group, under which Tyroo was spun off as a new company. Importantly, what it offered to us was a mental 'unlock'. It was this unlock that later enabled us to go ahead and launch more businesses under the new entity, one of them being the first meta search engine in India for flights, Zoomtra.

Three Million Dollars

'Congratulations! The tech due diligence has been cleared. We would like to invest three million dollars in the company,' we were told over a phone call by Yahoo, leaving us in awe. It truly was a magical year and everything that we were touching seemed to be turning into gold and we were truly grateful for it.

The only catch with this deal was that Yahoo wanted to acquire a 51 per cent stake. This one time we didn't want to sell a majority stake while already having done it with Quasar. Fortunately, we were able to settle the matter when Yahoo agreed to own a 49 per cent stake in Tyroo, leaving the balance 51 per cent to us.

The way the Yahoo deal was inked is also a story in itself. The lawyers at both ends had been going through all the clauses in the SHA with a fine-tooth comb for months, until they came upon the eve of the founding day of Yahoo. It so happened that Yahoo was keen to make the formal announcement of the deal on their founding day. The SHA that had been under discussion for months got signed in a matter of hours with a deadline looming large. It was nearly 10 p.m. when we were asked to put our signatures on the deal and send a copy across. With no one else available in the office, Harish couldn't figure out how to switch on the office printer to be able to scan the signed document. Till today, it remains a standing joke among us that we have the Yahoo deal available only by way of a JPEG file with a signature pasted on it

As the signing was done late at night, the announcement had to be made the next day. Harish's friend was the Food and Beverage head at ITC. He agreed to turn the iconic restaurant, Dum Pukht, into a press conference venue in the morning, at a small cost. That is where the Tyroo–Yahoo deal was formally announced.

It was nothing short of miraculous that within a year, we had turned into poster boys of the media industry with two large deals under our belts. In hindsight, what really helped us along our journey was the power of a dream. While we were still miles away from realizing it fully, the fact remained that, had we not harboured a dream or given up on it any sooner, we wouldn't have gotten this far. It was highly probable that we would have been content with becoming WPP employees and would have remained a one-trick pony at best. It was the power of this audacious dream that had allowed us to create structures to further unlock our potential. That, and the fact that God had been incredibly kind in allowing us to be at the right time and the right place!

Actionable Insights

The mechanics of an 'exit': A profitable business exit is an exciting occasion for the business and its stakeholders. There is no way that you want it to be the end of your entrepreneurial journey and/or regret it later. First things first, ensure that your reason to exit the business are robust. While personal wealth creation or astronomical business value are attractive reasons, they cannot be the most important ones. Here are some scenarios to consider and a viable strategy for each of them:

You love coming to work everyday	Business is healthy today	Future potential is bright and healthy	Actions
Yes	Yes	Yes	Don't think of exiting. Grow and grab more market share. Think of raising more capital for growth. PE / VC / IPO can be a few sources of capital.

You love coming to work everyday	Business is healthy today	Future potential is bright and healthy	Actions
Yes	Yes	No	Explore the possibility of a strategic acquisition to enhance future potential / look for funds to build a future proof adjacent business. You can also consider a merger / JV opportunity. Exit the business in case you aren't able to achieve either.
Yes	No	Yes	Explore the possibility of external fundraising to support current business health and future growth. If that isn't a possibility, focus on the cash flow. Cutting expenses even at the cost of reducing growth

You love coming to work everyday	Business is healthy today	Future potential is bright and healthy	Actions
			or sacrificing revenue may be important in this scenario.
No	Yes / No	Yes	Look for a competent leader for the business through internal growth or professional hire. Let the new leader decide on a future course while you take on a shareholder position and remain on the board. If this does not seem viable, exiting the business may be a feasible option.
Yes	No	No	Exit the business by way of strategic acquisition or a joint venture.

All in all, the reasons for an exit should be crystal clear and well thought out. Once you have made up your mind to exit the business in a healthy situation, remember that honest and bold conversations are key. The important bit is not to be overawed and ensure that you do not undersell. This advice, of course, does not hold if you are making a distress call where timely oxygen (read: capital) is a priority over deal optimization.

Even though every industry or company goes through different exit opportunity cycles, exiting in a bearish market or at the start of the bull cycle isn't the best way forward. After three business exits, this is one of the most important lessons that I have learnt. Instead, hold on, play out for the up-cycle and try to time it well.

Steer Clear from Minority Ownerships

As a thumb rule, it is best to undertake either a minority sale or a full sale. Selling (not valid for fundraising) a large majority and retaining a minority ownership works well only if the founder is able to mentally detach himself and is ready to work as an executive on day-to-day affairs.

In closing, it is important to remember that while exits can create personal wealth, sometimes they can also turn out to be the ultimate blank page for an entrepreneur.

Businesses are platforms that have a certain momentum and value. With exits, the whole platform is lost and the momentum ceases. Ensure, therefore, that you undertake exits for the right reasons. Importantly, post-exit, ensure that you retain the founder's mentality and are ready to hit the 'start' function again, driven by a sense of renewed purpose.

Chapter 8

A Dream Run . . . and a Jolt

Two Companies

If someone had predicted that we would be running two companies in a matter of a year, I am sure we would have laughed it off as a figment of their imagination. Yet this is exactly how life turned out to be.

The way the Quasar deal with WPP was structured, we stood to earn a large earnout, on the basis of the profit earned by the company. Our aim was therefore to grow the company and maximize our earnings. It worked well for us that Harish, C.P. and I had our jobs cut out—I handled the domestic digital media business, C.P. dealt with the tech services business while Harish took care of building the business globally. We had individual departments and teams but they were fully integrated and aligned. Overall, the company ran like well-oiled machinery. Along the way, we forged several joint ventures that further strengthened the Quasar story. The opportunity of a first international JV, in fact, was created when Harish and our colleague, Gopikaa, were travelling to Kenya to meet Scangroup, Africa's leading marketing and communication group, for potential business. A JV between Scangroup, Quasar and WPP, led to the birth of SQUAD (Scan + Quasar). It went on to become one of the leading agencies in Kenya with all the effort Harish and Gopikaa put towards this partnership. Another important partnership was established with Ogilvy One, another WPP company. Gopikaa, in fact, went on to play an integral role in leading the Global Business at Quasar, rising through the ranks to become its CEO. She began her journey as a fresher at StudioSmile, where she laid the foundation for her impressive career. Quasar's world-class key team members—including Piyush, Richa, Moneka, Ajay, Kamal, Manish, Vijay, Naresh, Aarti, and others—along with the founding team, were united on a shared mission. In all of this, what was also on the rise was our learning curve, as we were witnessing first-hand how large companies were run.

While Quasar was having a dream run, things at Tyroo were stable, though not quite as buoyant. For one, we didn't have complete clarity at this point on whether Yahoo would limit itself to the role of a financial stakeholder or emerge as a strategic partner. As Quasar was consuming a lot of our time, we had given the reins of Tyroo to Hitesh Dhingra and subsequently to Aditya Khanna. Aditya and I went back a long way, with our first meeting serendipitously taking place at a GMAT coaching institute that I had enrolled myself in during my stint at Rediff. While the GMAT coaching took a back seat when my entrepreneurial dreams soared, the relationship with Aditya went beyond the confines of the institute. It was another chance meeting with Aditya in Mumbai that led to his being a part of Tyroo. Aditya, to his credit, dropped his admission to Indian School of Business (ISB) to continue running Tyroo.

Rs 101

Around this time, while we were neck-deep in work, it so happened that there was a sealing drive on commercial establishments in the area where our office was located. Zamrudpur was classified under 'Lal Dora'—a legacy land classification system specific to Delhi, indicating a village residential area. It was clear that amidst our work commitments, we needed to look for a new office space. We were finding it hard to take the decision to invest in a space since it would significantly impact our earnings. At this time we were bailed out of the situation by an unexpected source—the mothers of the three co-founders. They decided to purchase the space and lease it out to us, turning themselves into our landlords. This way they built their rental income and we built our own office.

In our search for an office space that would fit the bill, my father happened to come across a space in Udyog Vihar, a well-known industrial estate in Gurgaon. Owned by one H.M. Singh (a kind gentleman who ran his engineering company from there and was now shifting to a bigger set-up in Chandigarh), the place seemed just right for our requirement. Quasar had by now grown to a 100+ team, and the number was on the rise, while Tyroo was also building up.

'*Sardarji, ye lijiye 101 rupay, deal pukki. Baat paise ki nahi, zubaan ki hai* (Sardarji, please accept Rs 101, and agree on the deal. It's not about money, but about giving one's word),' my father said, offering Mr Singh Rs 101 as a token of confirmation of the deal. I had seen my father follow this tradition whenever he bought any property, irrespective of its size. His logic was impeccable—for someone whose ethics were questionable, even crores were no guarantee that he wouldn't back out from a deal, while someone who was firm in character would never go back even if you had handed over Rs 101, he had maintained. Clearly H.M. Singh belonged to the latter category for he went on to honour the deal.

What was left now was to do up the space to meet our requirements, a task that we took on upon ourselves. '*Grey glass lagwao, sir. aajkal bahot trend mein hai* (Sir, please put in grey glass. It's the in thing),' the architect in charge, advised us to go with grey glass in the window panes. '*Glass toh blue hi lagenge, wo kya hai na, jab hum sapne mein apna office dekhte the, uski khidkiyan blue hua karti thi* (The glasses need to be blue; when we used to dream of having our own office building, the windows were always blue),' came Harish's reply. Those manifested dreams were finally coming true. To top it all, when it was time for us to move into the office, the inauguration was undertaken by none other than Martin Sorrell, the big boss of WPP.

The office did bring us a lot of luck as Quasar experienced unprecedented growth in the time we operated from there. All of us believed that it was made possible on account of a virtuous circle of blessings—especially the blessings of our moms—the fiercest landlords we could have had—who warned us that their rent shouldn't be delayed by a day beyond the agreed seventh day of every month.

Cracks in the Partnership

'There is an opportunity. Let's discuss it,' Harish barged into the new office one day excitedly. Apparently, he had met someone from Europe, through a friend. This person wanted to partner on an e-commerce business in India. This was in 2009. The recent financial crisis had focused global attention on new infrastructure development that could facilitate the digital economy. In fact, billions of Internet and mobile users globally had begun to make a strong case for huge opportunities in the e-commerce and m-commerce space. India too was ripe to partake of this development.

Harish proposed that we call for a board meeting to discuss the proposal. The said board meeting was attended by Harish, C.P. and me, as well as Mr Swaroop who, other than being a mentor, had assumed the role of the Chairman of the company.

'We need to invest an amount to enter the e-commerce space for this partnership.' Harish started the meeting by pointing this out. While we had made money in the Quasar–WPP deal, the quoted amount felt like a huge investment. We had all come from middle-class backgrounds and somewhere we were still shy of taking big bets. Besides, we were going through the global financial crisis of 2009 and it only felt prudent that we should focus on the money on the table—namely, Quasar's earnout. Little surprise then that Harish was met with a number of questions and clarifications while the proposal that Harish had received demanded that the decision be taken fairly quickly.

The bigger constraint than the time, as we discovered in the meeting, was that once you encounter success, even erstwhile hustlers can show a tendency to slow down and question each other. It was no different for us. Besides, our risk appetites were quite different. Harish was extremely aspirational and an aggressive risk-taker. People's impression of me, however, was that I looked both ways on a street that had one-way traffic, before crossing the road. As the proverbial calculating risk taker, I always wanted to be able to see things clearly before making a move. I felt that I needed more information to be able to make an informed decision.

When the proposal was put to the vote in the board meeting, therefore, the nays exceeded the yeas, and the investment idea was shot down by a majority vote. The meeting, however, concluded with a remark that we could relook at the proposal if the investment amount could be significantly brought down or else Harish could go ahead and execute this deal alone.

While the voting, among the four of us, settled the issue at hand, it raked up a bigger issue. Harish particularly was left feeling quite frustrated at what he saw as an apparent lack of aspiration. On the personal front, he felt as if his wings had been clipped. Whether our (lack of) investment decision turned out to be right or wrong only time would tell; one thing was certain—we had unwittingly sown the seeds of discontent in our partnership on account of our varied aspirations. Thankfully, through it all, our friendship remained strong.

Actionable Insights

Navigating the co-founder relationship: Entrepreneurship is an intense, lonely and hard journey. It is best if you have a partner to scale the peaks and valleys together. Having a partner who has a similar value system, passion and complementary skills, makes a world of difference.

That said, co-founder relationships are a lot like marriages in terms of their intensity. No matter how well you get along, how aligned your vision is or how complementary your skills are, there will be times when you have different opinions or expectations. How you handle these situations can make or break your co-founder relationship.

I have been lucky to have my business partner for over 20 + years, even though we have had our share of ups and downs. Some of the things that we have been mindful of include:

- It is best to restrict the number of co-founders to two or maximum three. Anything more than that can lead to inefficient decision making and can also lead to friction. Splitting the equity equally if co-founders are joining at the time of incorporation and setting up a vesting schedule for co-founders at the time of joining are other areas to pay attention to.

- There is no space for 'I' in a partnership. It's the 'we' that needs to rule. Sentiments like 'I do more than you' or 'I own more than you' spell doom.

- It helps to identify who among the co-founders will be the final decision maker. In my opinion co-CEOs or no-CEO is a recipe for disaster. You can go ahead and debate issues fiercely. When it comes to the final decision-making, however, allow the designated CEO the room to take decisions and then offer your wholehearted support.

- With success comes fame (often 15 minutes of fame). That's when you need to be most careful. Decide in advance, on who will be the public spokesperson of the company so that there is no confusion or underlying dissatisfaction. The media is a double-edged sword. Just as you need to learn to handle fame, you need to navigate times of negative press as a team.

- Remember, if the co-founders are separated by an inch, the teams below, are separated by a mile. Therefore, keep a continuous focus on common alignment of mission, vision and strategy.

- The one thing co-founders cannot afford to pay any attention to is the grapevine. There will be enough instances where there will be rumours, gossip mongering, a game of Chinese Whispers and more. Instead of making any impressions or taking decisions based on the grapevine, it always works best to seek clarifications immediately straight from the horse's mouth.

- All founders should, ideally, have the ability to manage their temperament during high pitched emotional discussions and stay clear from 'one door decisions' in such situations.

- It is important to grow individually and together. The individual growth of each co-founder in their respective responsibility areas is important so that there isn't a gap between their exposure and vision.

- Last but not the least, travel together. Create possibilities of engagement amongst yourselves and your respective families.

Chapter 9

New Beginnings

'I have done the e-commerce deal as it was time sensitive.'

Harish declared one morning. To his credit, Harish had proposed this deal to the partnership first and had suggested that everyone come on board and invest.

While I fully empathized with his point of view, the fact that he was venturing out on the e-commerce project alone, left me wondering if the situation could have been handled differently by us.

We were, of course, mature enough to not let this come in the way of our friendship and our partnership.

It was around this time that I happened to reconnect with Hitesh Dhingra. One of the first three team members at Quasar and an early leader at Tyroo, Hitesh had now launched an e-commerce company, Letsbuy.com, that sold electronic products. Hitesh was running the company out of a 200-square-feet office in central Delhi's Patel Nagar. 'I sold one floor of our paternal home to fund this company,' Hitesh told me as he shared his start-up story. His statement left me in awe; the fact that he had taken this kind of a personal risk to fund his start-up, convinced me that he had skin in the game. *'E-commerce bahot bada hone wala hai, sir. Aap bhi aa jao* (E-commerce is going to be big. You come too). We will have an early mover advantage,' he said. I was in any case on the fence when Harish had made the suggestion of investing in the e-commerce business. With Hitesh's conviction I was prompted to look at it more positively. 'What is the investment you would require me to bring to the table?' I asked him. 'You can invest whatever you like. I really want to have you as a partner. I have learnt a lot from you and I want that journey to continue,' came his reply. It was mutual respect for each other that prompted me to take out Rs 101 from my wallet and offer it at the small temple that Hitesh had set up in his office, as a sign of my commitment. I went on to invest a few lakhs in Letsbuy. com, acquiring a 26 per cent stake in the company, which had one more co-founder, Amanpreet (Aman) Bajaj.

NROOC

If on the one hand, our e-commerce journeys were just about beginning, one could best describe Tyroo as experiencing a slow burn at the time. While the company wasn't bleeding, it didn't really seem to be headed anywhere. So far, while we had been caught up with the Quasar growth story, somewhere each of us had also nursed this disappointment that we had not been able to convert Tyroo into a big success. By this time, the space had also seen the entry of a number of other players—InMobi, Komli—all of whom had received large funding rounds.

'Go big or go home,' that was broadly the theme of the board meeting that was called to discuss the way forward for

Tyroo. 'We have the money that we raised from Yahoo. Let us use that money to create a buzz for Tyroo, while we raise more funds'—that was pretty much the consensus that was emerging in the meeting. But my heart was not in this suggestion. I didn't want to use the money till we had a clear plan in sight. The idea of spraying and praying—spending the money without really knowing where we were headed—didn't really appeal to me. While the proposal for spending that money was being put to vote, I was reminded of a session that I had attended that had Eric Schmidt, the former CEO of Google, as a speaker. When the moderator asked him what his biggest entrepreneurial learning had been, each of us waited with bated breath, certain that he would have lots to say. Instead, he surprised us with five letters. 'NROOC,' he said. When prompted further, he explained that the acronym stood for Never Run out of Cash. Several companies, Schmidt explained, had been killed on account of negative cash flows. While a company could be earning profits, it could still die if it had negative cash flows. On the other hand, you could be running into losses, but if you have cash flows on your side, you could turn things around, ran his argument. NROOC, as a concept, has stayed with me ever since and I was convinced that it was time to put it into practice. I therefore voted against spending the money we had in Tyroo without a solid plan, a decision that worked well for us, especially as several other changes were in the offing.

Come 2010, and an important piece of news awaited us. We were approached by Keith Nilsson and David Gowdey, erstwhile leaders of Yahoo's Corporate Development Group, to inform us that they were leaving Yahoo! to start a new venture capital fund, called Xplorer Capital that would be focused on emerging markets investments. As part of their first investments, they had made an agreement with Yahoo's management to purchase the minority investments that Yahoo! had made in the emerging markets, many of which were in Asia. By this time, we had already taken the decision of giving Tyroo our best shot. We therefore decided to take this opportunity to increase our equity in Tyroo from the existing 51 per cent to as much as 65 per cent, while offering the rest of it to Xplorer Capital. What made this decision easier for us was also the fact that by this time we had maximized our earnout in Quasar. While we were still 25 per cent owners of the company, our obligation to work there, full-time, had nearly ended (even though we continued to function as board members until 2017).

At this time, Harish was busy expanding his e-commerce venture that was looking at horizontal growth with the launch of several e-commerce verticals. C.P, meanwhile, wanted to take a back seat, selling his equity in Tyroo, to us. As for me, I felt that I could now put time and energy behind Tyroo and Letsbuy.com. While Harish and I had separate e-commerce ventures, we continued to work together with Tyroo as our major focus area, with me taking over the reins as the CEO of Tyroo.

Fortunately for me, in taking over Tyroo's day-to-day operations, I had the support of an able team in the duo of Siddharth Puri and Ashwani Mehta. These were team members who were fully invested in the company. In fact, Siddharth, who had joined Tyroo as an executive and had risen through the ranks, had, on one occasion, sought me out, imploring me to look closely at Tyroo's operations. But at the time, I was neck-deep in maximizing the earnout at Quasar and I wasn't of much help. I had never, however, been able to forget Siddharth's tear-filled eyes. '*Tyroo ko sambhal lo, nahi toh band ho jayegi* (Save Tyroo or it will sink),' he had said then. It was now time to live up to this promise.

Actionable Insights

Never run out of cash: Reports show that a whopping 38 per cent of businesses fail because they run out of cash.[1] A lot of companies raise capital and then spend most of it to buy growth, only to be able to raise the next round of capital. While there is nothing wrong in this approach, however, one of the biggest responsibilities of a founder is to ensure that the company doesn't get to a point of capital starvation. To this end, here are some principles that have worked in my journey:

Forget 25 per cent of the total capital raised

While you optimize fundraising, one of the immediate steps to follow is to run your business believing that you have raised only 75 per cent of the capital. Now that means that you either raise the next round of capital before it hits this reserve or make changes to the business economics and prepare to become cash flow positive. Either way do not bring the business to a point where it is down to having a few weeks or months of cash.

---

[1] 'The Top 20 Reasons Startups Fail', *CB Insights*, 16 December 2024, https://www.cbinsights.com/research/report/startup-failure-reasons-to

Cash Flow vs Profit & Loss (P&L)

Keep an eye on the monthly (or weekly) cash flow statement of the company as much as you monitor the monthly P&L. Along with the cash flow and P&L, the 'net cash position' will help you to manage the runway of the company. As far as possible break down the P&L by department or product or geography as it suits the business. A word of caution here—responsible cash flow management implies never delaying employee salaries or vendor payments. Not only is this ethically correct, it also helps build credibility while ensuring that the discipline of your own collections is maintained.

I often say that if you want to learn 'cash flow' management, our mothers are our best teachers. They dexterously manage their opex (monthly expenses), capex (extraordinary expenses) and reserves (the cash most women keep on the side for emergencies). It will help to remember that frugality is a value system and should not be confused with being miserly.

Cap table management

Be mindful of your cap table structures. Not only do founders lose interest when they have low equity in the company, it could also come in the way of your funding. Another area to be mindful of is not to offer free equity to non-executive co-founders or advisors. Instead, get everyone to invest capital even if it is at a discount on the current share price. This allows them to have some skin in the game.

Chapter 10

LetsBuy

Note: The subsequent chapters speak of the funding process at LetsBuy and make a reference to seven Venture Capital (VC) firms. Since the events are being narrated by me and the POV is entirely mine, it is only fair that I mask the names of the VCs. I am sure that they had their own reasons for taking the decisions that they did; reasons which I may not have been privy to. My aim isn't to sensationalize any of their decisions/events as I continue to hold investors in high esteem. While I have tried to reproduce these events, which are over a decade old, faithfully, any discrepancy in timelines is inadvertent.

Last but not the least, I would want to offer an apology to the reader who will need to go through the maze of these VC firms being addressed numerically.

Visit to Your Office

That was the subject line of an email that hit our mailboxes one day. Sent by the super boss of a large hedge fund (let us call them VC One for convenience), the email was destined to change the course of operations at LetsBuy.

Ever since I had decided to invest in the company, Hitesh had sought my help to raise funds, a task that I had taken to actively. As part of the fundraising process, we visited a few

Indian investors and found most of them questioning how big
e-commerce could become in India. While we, as co-founders,
could see the big picture, we needed the backing of an investor
who believed in the future of the industry.

This was one of the reasons why hearing from VC One,
the largest in the space, was exciting. This VC was investing
aggressively in India's small but growing e-commerce space
and literally shaping it. Flipkart, for one, which was still in its
first avatar, selling books at the time, had received a round of
funding from them.

The super boss's email, expressing a desire to visit our
small 200-square-feet office at Patel Nagar, had driven us into
a tizzy. 'Subah 9.30 toh hamara peon bhi nahi aata (even our
peon doesn't come at 9.30 a.m.),' Hitesh said, wondering how
we would pull off the early morning visit. True to Hitesh's
fears, when the person concerned made his way up the small
winding staircase of the office—reaching forty-five minutes
before his scheduled time—the office was still being swept and
tidied. The young, astute investor, who was at the top of his
game, however, didn't waste any time and promptly decided
that we would need a better venue for our discussion. 'Is there
a hotel around?' he asked politely. The venue of the meeting
was thus changed to the nearby hotel, Jaypee Siddharth, where
we continued our conversation. Once Hitesh described the
LetsBuy journey, the investor pulled out a writing pad from the
stack in the hotel's conference room and drew a pyramid with

some deft strokes. He explained to us how he had witnessed the growth of e-commerce companies across the world. 'In India these companies can be divided into three tiers,' he said, while dividing the pyramid he had drawn into three parts with a firm hand. 'Companies that are witnessing twenty to thirty orders a day; those that are serving fifty to hundred orders a day and those that are at 100 orders plus. I am looking at companies that are in the third bracket with over 100 orders a day,' he declared, with a flourish. 'I like you guys,' he added, 'but I need 100 orders a day to make an investment decision,' he said, with the confidence of someone who knew his job.

At that time, LetsBuy was serving an average of thirty orders a day. While we didn't fit into his investment bracket, meeting him had given us a clear goal. We had to reach the target of 100. To be able to scale ourselves up from thirty to 100 orders, however, wasn't going to be easy. To complicate matters, we only had Rs 30 lakh in our bank account to achieve this. We weren't ready to give up.

Having quickly returned to the drawing board to figure out some strategies to achieve this number, our first attempt was to try to get some free media publicity for the website. Parallely, we also tried to get the electronics brands we were signing up with, to promote the fact that their products were available at LetsBuy. Hitesh also managed to crack a deal with SBI where SBI not only promoted our partnership at their ATMs, SBI customers could also use their loyalty points to make purchases on LetsBuy. Slowly, we saw our numbers inching up. We were now a twelve-people team with Rs 70 lakh in monthly sales and found ourselves breaking even.

At each step, we kept the potential investor updated about our order numbers through fortnightly mails. We wanted him to know how seriously we were chasing the target he had set for us. Whether or not we hit the target, he would definitely know that it wasn't from lack of trying. It was around the time that our orders finally hit 100 a day, that we received yet another email from him stating that he was visiting India and that he would be happy to meet us. Having learnt a lesson, the hard way from trying to host the previous meeting at our office, we fixed the erstwhile Aman Hotel, at Lodhi Road, as the venue for this meeting. The meeting was also to be attended by VC Two, another marquee investment firm. Not one to beat around the bush, the super boss at VC One started the meeting by telling us that he was now ready to invest in our company and asked us for a number that we were looking for by way of investment. '4 million dollars,' we instantly retorted. He left us with 'Let me come back to you,' causing us to wonder if we had gone overboard.

A couple of days went by before we received yet another email informing us that he would like to have another conversation with us. Good news awaited us at the other end of the bridge number that was the norm in holding conference calls in those days. 'We have decided to invest in LetsBuy,' came his booming voice over the call. Even before we could heave a sigh of relief, his next sentence gave us a bit of a scare. 'We will, however, not give you the 4 million dollars you have asked for,' he said, leaving us worried about what we would be able to achieve with the amount he was about to suggest, e-commerce being a cost-intensive business. 'We will give you 7.5 million dollars instead,' he added. For a split second, we wondered if we had heard him correctly. It turned out that we had, as he started explaining that his experience in China had helped him realize that e-commerce required the kind of investment he was suggesting. We were barely able to gather our wits together on this huge upside, to be able to tell him that while the figure of $7.5 million sounded good, it would be hard for us to accept it since we couldn't look at a higher dilution than what we had already committed to. What he had to say next was something we couldn't have ever anticipated. 'We will offer you 7.5 million dollars for the same dilution.'

However, he put down three conditions. His first condition was that we should go deeper in the electronics vertical before we decide to expand to other areas. It made tremendous business sense for us to go in for vertical growth, before taking a horizontal growth model, and we agreed immediately. His next condition was that the investment was contingent on the fact that I should continue my role with the business. He was aware that I had invested in the business and was more like a shadow partner. His third and final condition was that Amanpreet, who was then serving his notice period at Ernst & Young, join full-time formally as the third co-founder, something that was already in the offing. We accepted all three conditions. This investment was a huge validation for a company that had been set up by Hitesh at a time when no one had any template for an e-commerce model for India. As for me, it also reinforced confidence in my ownself.

'Why don't you take on the role of the CEO of the company?' I was approached by VC Two, a few days after this call. 'This is Hitesh's baby. I won't be the CEO but I will also not shy away from any responsibility,' I said upfront. 'I have no problem at all, sir. In fact, it would be great if you took on the mantle of the CEO,' Hitesh, tried to convince me. I, however, stood firm since in my mind, the CEO role was his to take. Besides, I had already given my commitment to lead Tyroo as its CEO. 'E-commerce is a much larger game. You should consider spending more time with LetsBuy,'-advised my friend, Deep Kalra, the founder of MakeMyTrip. The emotional baggage of Tyroo that I was carrying, however, did not allow me to accept his advice. 'I love the digital media sector; I think I will just stick to that industry,' I reiterated. In hindsight, what all of them were predicting about the e-commerce space did turn out to be true, given the explosive growth that the segment witnessed.

With their conditions met, VC One, VC Two and VC Three, jointly participated in a 7.5-million-dollar investment round that gave LetsBuy a huge push. One of the first things that we did was to move to a new office. This one, located at Adhchini, in Delhi, had earlier been the office of MakeMyTrip and had been a witness to its huge growth. One of the other things in its favour was that the office precinct offered us an opportunity to put up a huge signboard, displaying the LetsBuy name and logo, one that we were committed to take to newer heights.

Actionable Insights

Story rules: Investor and author Morgan Housel rightly said, 'Every investment price, every market valuation is just a number from today multiplied by a story about tomorrow.' As an entrepreneur, you need to tell your story well. This does not mean that you need to spin tales but that you need to know how to present facts and to deliver them with emotion. To that extent, storytelling is a key entrepreneurial skill. Some people are born story tellers, for others it's a learnable skill. You have to be your company's top sales person whether it is to investors, to your team, clients or partners. Ensure your story is simple, engaging and impactful.

Take risks, not chances: A recent web series made the phrase, '*Risk hai toh ishq hai* (if there is risk, there is love)' very popular. There is no denying that entrepreneurship involves taking risks at every step. So much so that in the context of entrepreneurship, risk is what's left over after you think you've thought of everything. As much as possible, take calculated risks by investing in preparedness. Above everything, plan like a pessimist even as you dream like an optimist.

Product or GTM: A common mistake made by first time entrepreneurs is to put the product ahead of go-to-market (GTM) in terms of priority during the formative years of the company. They really need to go hand-in hand. In fact, I will stick my neck out and even dare to say that you need to prioritize GTM over your product early on. GTM strategy evolves out of trial and error and is expensive. It is therefore imperative that you start working on it early. In fact, it is important that you find the company's area of success in terms of its positioning, impact and ideal customer profile (ICP) quickly.

Chapter 11

High on Adrenaline

We had literally been transformed into adrenaline junkies during this period. There was a lot of excitement at work as we were onboarding new brands on the site every single day, besides witnessing an increase in traffic as well as a surge in average orders per day. With the move to the new office and the money in our bank, we were also able to hire great talent. 'Optimizing for the best electronics store' became our North Star Metric in the months to come, one that we were determined to achieve.

The process of setting up and scaling an e-commerce business, however, was no mean task, as we needed to play on several aspects, the most important being the price. Besides, these were the early days of e-commerce in India and hence a lot of time and energy was also spent in building technology in-house, as the suite of tools, platforms and software solutions, as we know them today, were virtually non-existent. Hitesh, Aman and our founding team spent several nights in the office, working on all these issues.

Over and above the operational aspects, a major learning for us was that e-commerce is a business of scale and that until you hit a certain threshold number, you cannot hope to make profits. On the other hand, since category creation demanded offering customers jaw-dropping prices, it actually meant losing money on every single order. If we had thought we could make the business profitable with the funding that we had raised, we soon realized that it was not to be. E-commerce was a high bleed business. Period.

Two Supercars

Sometime in January 2011, we were approached by the leaders of the largest e-commerce company in the world. They wanted to understand the e-commerce explosion in India and were keen for a possible strategic partnership, investment or acquisition. While we had a very warm conversation, we were so deep in the process of building our company that we didn't think of it as an option. Our view was that we would build the largest e-commerce company in India, instead of giving way to the largest of the world. The discussion, however, gave us a huge amount of confidence that we were headed in the right direction.

As things progressed, within nine to ten months of raising our first round, we approached VC One, Two and Three once again for yet another round of funding. In our meeting with them, VC One, having also made an investment in Flipkart, was quite upfront with their point of view. 'Funding both Flipkart and you is like funding two supercars that may soon race against each other,' they reasoned. Their decision, therefore, was that while they were willing to put in additional funds, they didn't want to become the lead investor in the round.

With VC One hesitant to lead the funding round, we felt the need to find a big boy to step in as our lead investor. By this time, our valuation had already hit twenty times of what we had started out with. A number of other VCs were therefore showing interest. Before we knew it, we had two term sheets—a combined term sheet from two big VCs (VC Four and Five, for convenience) and another one from yet another leading venture capital firm, a rather large name in the space (VC Six). I was inclined to go ahead with the former combo as I felt that there was a better fit in terms of the overall approach to business. It worked well that Hitesh and Aman were happy to go along with my decision. Together we decided to keep the term sheet of VC Six on hold, as we continued to negotiate the joint terms offered by VC Four and Five.

Word, however, reached VC Six that we were negotiating with the two others. Not one to leave issues unresolved, they instantly reached out to the other VCs asking them to intervene. Before I knew it, we were summoned for a meeting with VC Four. The venue for the meeting, Costa Coffee at SDA market, opposite IIT Delhi, could well be considered a start-up adda, especially as it was visited by a lot of aspirants from IIT Delhi. If you passed by the tables, you could hear several different start-up ideas being discussed.

'Why aren't you taking the discussion ahead with VC Six?' they asked, just as we settled down with our coffees. Next thing

I knew, we were being counselled by them that it was in the company's interest to have all three of them come together in the funding round. 'Together we will be a force. Don't worry about anything,' we were reassured. Even though we were worried about having too many VC partners on the cap table, since we were looking at raising a large funding round somewhere in the range of mid-double-digit million dollars, we went with their suggestion. What prompted us to agree to this arrangement was also the meeting arranged by VC Six with one of their global partners, a well regarded figure of the VC world, who had flown down from the US to meet a few Indian founders, probably in his private plane. We have one silver bullet to fire in the Indian e-commerce space and we want to fire it with you guys, he said to us. The awe of interacting with a doyen of the industry finally led us to agree to their participation, despite my initial apprehensions. The fact that our previous VC partners were also participating in the round was, in any case, a huge vote of confidence in our favour.

We were at this time preparing for the Diwali of 2011, the time of the year when India stares at a bumper festive shopping season. It was imperative that we get in the funding early to be able to encash on the season. We suggested therefore that the three new VCs on the cap table contribute $12.5 million each while we raise the balance from existing investors, taking the round upto $42.5 million. The stage seemed to be set for us to up our game with the VCs ready to sign a term sheet, only we didn't know any better at the time.

Actionable Insights

Follow your gut: An old saying, '*Suno sabki, karo man ki* (listen to everyone; do what you think is right)' stands the test of time. When you have heard everyone's opinion, take the final call based on First Principle Thinking, i.e., boiling a process down to its fundamental parts, a business-first attitude and, above all, by listening to your gut. Start-ups are by nature agile and iterative. Its decision-making cannot be any less. The framework below has helped me decide which decisions have to be made quickly versus which ones require slow, careful thought.

1. Two-way door decisions: These are decisions that can be reversed without much impact. These decisions can be taken quickly because you can always come back if you find that something isn't working. They provide opportunities to experiment, learn and iterate.

2. One-way door decisions: These are decisions that have lasting effects and are often hard to reverse. Joint ventures, shutting down a business unit, getting in a co-founder etc fall under this category and need a lot of evaluation.

A word of caution here. While you may go wrong on several decisions despite the most careful evaluation, not taking any decisions for fear of making the wrong decisions, of course, may be the worst sort of decision making.

Surround support: We are all starved for cash in the early stages of entrepreneurship and we tend to optimize on most costs. Amidst all this, it is important to remember not to compromise on regulatory stuff. Be it your lawyer, your chartered accountant, tax advisory firm, company secretary, marketing agency, etc., any kind of surround support has to be the best-in-class. This does not necessarily mean going with the most expensive names in the industry. What it does mean is to make the choice carefully, after evaluating their expertise. Beyond making the choice of firm, also choose the person you would be working with. A fair balance between expertise and availability of the professional can be a good guiding principle.

Valuation versus value: Who doesn't love a high valuation? However, it is the fine balance between valuation and the value that an investor brings to the table, that is key. Importantly, the investor needs to be aligned to the value system of the enterprise. In my opinion, up to 15 per cent valuation can be ignored should you feel that the investor comes with a great track record and that there is an alignment on the value system.

Chapter 12

Hard Lessons

While we were excited to receive the term sheet, one of its terms caught us completely off guard. It stated that the company needed to be registered offshore. As entrepreneurs who came from humble backgrounds and who had only made an entry into the e-commerce space, such a concept was not just alien but also scary. 'Why would we do that?' we asked, only to be told that it would open up a host of opportunities in terms of inviting capital as also for a potential listing of the company on the NASDAQ at a later date. We were not so convinced. To be fair to them, it wasn't an outlandish suggestion as other companies were going through a similar process. As a company, however, we were not ready for it at this stage. In fact, the suggestion, in some ways, validated my fears of going ahead with an investor whose approach to business wasn't complementary to ours.

What we were also extremely concerned about was the timing. We didn't want to miss the opportunity that would present itself during Diwali. Even with the little information we had about global funding, we knew that it was a time-consuming process. In our desperation, we reached out to experts for help. One of the people we turned to for counsel was a trusted advisor, who worked at one of the Big Four audit companies. It was he who suggested that we speak to a law firm.

He also put us in touch with a partner in his personal capacity, at a renowned law firm, probably among India's top two.

The partner concerned at the law firm not only kindly agreed to speak to me in good faith, he also spent a lot of time explaining stuff to me over an unpaid call. 'We are humble entrepreneurs, sir. We don't understand the concept of global company incorporations,' I said, sounding as desperate as I was feeling. While the gentleman explained to me that it wasn't an uncommon occurrence and that it was totally within the ambit of the law, he quizzed me on the 'why' of taking this decision. While I parroted the reasons offered to me, he left me with 'You need to have a solid 'why' before you make this decision.' Wanting to come to a final yes or no decision as time was running out, I asked him a final decisive question as we were about to end our call. *'Aap apne bete ko kya salah dete* (What advice would you have given your son)?' I asked, emboldened by the kindness shown by the gentleman, the best in his field. *'Main usse bolta, mat karo* (I would have told him not to do it). Your 'why' isn't convincing enough,' came his reply. That sealed the decision for me. Thanking the gentleman profusely, I set out to have a discussion with Hitesh and Aman. Together we were sure that we did not want to exercise this option.

It was now time to inform our investors about our decision. The video call that we undertook to convey our decision was attended by a battery of lawyers. 'We do not want to go ahead with the suggestion of registering an offshore company,' I began, only to be quizzed by them on the rationale. I tried to explain that we needed to be ready for the festive season and therefore had no time to spend on the process. To this, we were told that registering would take as little as one and a half months and wouldn't come in the way of our festive sales. I then went on to explain that our 'why' wasn't really convincing and that we were advised by several people in the industry not to go ahead. 'Who is advising you?' they asked, but I evaded the question. 'You may not be receiving advice from the right people and may land up making a bad decision,' they persisted. All this time, I was also repeatedly told that registering the company abroad was a good decision and that by not agreeing to it, we were coming in the way of the company's growth. It was the reiteration of this sentence, that we didn't know what was right for the company that we were painstakingly building, that made me sit up and think again. In hindsight, it was a case of being led by one's own limiting beliefs to think that investors who were sitting on millions of dollars knew much better about the business than an entrepreneur who was just starting out on his journey. Led by this belief, we finally took the one-way door decision of agreeing to register the company abroad for global funding. The one thing that I made sure of was to get them to agree to make $6 million available immediately at the signing of the term sheet so that the festive season wasn't compromised, while the registration process was put in process.

The matter sorted out, a light-hearted conversation followed, with each of us committing to put our best foot forward. It was in the midst of this seemingly well-intentioned discussion that I was casually asked where I had received the advice of not registering the company. In what seemed like a friendly discussion, now that all of us were on the same page, I told them the names of the people, maintaining that I was sharing their names in strict confidence and that the people concerned had gone out of their way to help us. It turned out that I couldn't have been more naive.

The next call that I received was from my contact at the audit firm, 'Manish, I haven't ever received a more humiliating call,' he said. Apparently, the lawyer of the VC firm called both the audit and the law firms, demanding to know in no uncertain terms how they could offer advice contrary to theirs. 'Do we give you business or do these entrepreneurs, I was asked point-blank,' he recounted. No amount of apology, I knew, would be enough to make good the harm I had unwittingly caused to them. Sure enough, my messages and mails of apology to the partner at the law firm did not elicit any response. I learnt a lesson the hard way that day.

On the business front, however, things were off to a good start. The termsheet signed, the promised $6 million came in, enabling us to cater to the festive demand. In fact, that Diwali we decided to take a giant leap and advertise on television for the first time, further expanding our reach. In making our TV debut with an India–England match, we had chosen to go with the 'C' of the A (Astrology), B (Bollywood), C (Cricket) and D (Devotional) combo that was a favourite of Indian audiences. We also went on to acquire a whole building and moved our office to a much larger space, besides also acquiring space for a large warehouse for our growing operations. It was a time when everyone in the business was passionately putting in more than required towards building the business. Our recruitment was also on in full swing, and before we knew it, we had more than 350 people working with us.

Within ten months of raising our first round of capital, we had grown our sales from Rs 70 lakh a month to Rs 28 crore a month and now had four regional warehouses.

Ironically, amidst all this seeming growth, if one was to look at the traditional parameters of business, our balance sheet was bleeding. In fact, every single transaction was adding to our loss. We had a negative Contribution Margin 3 (CM3), with options such as coupons, cashback and more being offered to entice customers. In fact, at a point in time, our monthly loss had accumulated to as much as Rs 1.5 crore, a staggering amount in those times. It sometimes made us wonder if we could even call what we were running a 'business' in the true sense of the term. The advice from people who knew how e-commerce worked, however, was *Dekho mat, bhagaate raho* (Just keep going)!' We continued to do just that, especially since our company valuation was on a steep growth path as we had emerged as the country's largest online electronics retailer. In fact, we were potentially, in some categories, selling cheaper even than the price offered by brands to their dealers. This was why we even had dealers and distributors from far-flung areas visiting our office and godowns to buy products.

Our SHA was also nearly stitched by now, even though negotiation conversations with lawyers had turned out to be extremely high-pressure. At one stage, one of our lawyers was reportedly in tears on what he described as 'demeaning conversations'. On our part, we had decided not to take any money from the company as a secondary sale of our equity. The company registration timelines had now arrived and it seemed that the company would be ready to receive its funds by early January 2012.

A Holiday

We had worked night and day in the last few months. While Hitesh and Aman had been involved in the operational running of the site tirelessly, I had been occupied with funding decisions and other strategic issues. In addition to LetsBuy, I was also running Tyroo at this time as its full-time CEO and had been neck-deep in work. As a hectic and eventful year drew to a close, I decided to unwind with a short holiday over a cruise trip in Singapore. 'I am headed to Singapore for a short vacation but will be available over a call for anything.' I thought it prudent to inform one of the partners from amongst the new VCs, as I stood in the immigration queue at New Delhi airport. The voice at the other end reassured me that everything was on track. At the time, we were awaiting the completion of the final registration formalities. All the financial and legal due diligence had already taken place and we were told it was only a matter of a few days before we received the funding in our accounts.

On the evening of December 20, the last day of my cruise, my attention was drawn to a conference call that was initiated by one of the new VC partners. I stepped out onto the balcony of the cruise ship and found myself staring at the limitless expanse. I had thought at the time that I would at best be attending to a last-minute sticky SHA clause. What the voice at the other end had to say, however, scared the living daylights out of me. I was told that e-commerce was a bleeding, capital guzzling business and that the partnership was getting extremely nervous as our business metrics had shown a sharp decline. His comments raised alarm bells in my head while through the glass door I could see my family enjoying the last evening aboard the cruise ship. They were, of course, oblivious to the fact that the seemingly innocuous call that I was attending to was about to change everything. The voice at the other end went on to suggest that we look at a smaller bridge round that would be put up for discussion with other VCs. The call was followed up with a detailed email setting out the issues that they saw in the metrics of the company.

We had set a whole machinery into motion—recruited people, acquired offices, put marketing plans in place. It was as if someone had pulled the rug out from under our feet. My worst fears seemed to be coming true. I wish I could undo a string of decisions that we had taken. Alas, that time was long gone.

Dark Christmas

It sure was a dark Christmas. I cut short the rest of my holiday and rushed back home. The intervening days were filled with huge rounds of discussions with the consortium of VCs Four, Five and Six. The other VCs, however, weren't comfortable with the proposed smaller bridge round as they felt it wouldn't work given the highly competitive e-commerce space. From having investors chase us, to us chasing them, life seemed to have come full circle.

The new year, however, showed us a flicker of hope. In early January, after several discussions, the consortium finally proposed a revised construct amounting to a round of $40 million at a 75 per cent reduced pre-money valuation. The precondition to which was also that new investors contributing to $14 million be inducted into the round. While we absorbed the new terms, we realized that it wouldn't be an easy task to look for new investors especially since time was of the essence.

Thus followed a mad scamper to reach out to every possible investor. The VC consortium, especially VC Four and VC Five, on their part were helpful in making some quick introductions that could help us pitch for the additional $14 million. One of the introductions that VC Four helped with, was to VC Seven. Their partner was also known to Nitin Gupta, my ex-boss at Rediff and now an angel investor in LetsBuy. On hearing of our plight and the fact that we were running out of time, he very kindly agreed that they would, for the time being, go with VC Four's due diligence and participate with $7 million, while the balance $7 million would come once they had undertaken their own due diligence. This process, they told us, was likely to take thirty to forty days. We heaved a sigh of relief. The problem was solved, or so we thought. I was in seventh heaven and the first thing I wanted to do was to call the investors and get going.

'Guys, the issue is resolved. We have stitched the new round together,' I beamed over a conference call, relief written all over my face. In my wildest dreams, I wasn't expecting the response that would follow. I was told by one of the consortium members that they had decided to stay away from the funding round given that the space was getting heated and that our business metrics were crumbling. To be fair to them, competition in the e-commerce space had indeed intensified, affecting our contribution margin. Our monthly burn rate was also up significantly to as much as Rs 6.5 crores while our monthly gross merchandise value, sales and customers were on the rise. That said, e-commerce was a winner-takes-all business and we needed to continue to invest if we had to build a category. We couldn't suddenly put all our efforts to a grinding halt. 'What are you saying?' I reasoned. 'This round was proposed just 15 days ago as an alternate to the old round', I reminded them. My arguments, however, fell on deaf ears. It was surreal. How could this happen, especially when everyone knew full well what impact this decision would have on our business?

The intervening days were a blur. I knew however that I couldn't give up just yet. I made one more attempt, this time to speak to the other VCs in the consortium to persuade them to go ahead, now that we had an additional commitment. However, with one of the consortium members withdrawing the others weren't inclined to go ahead either. As a last-ditch effort, I even attempted a final joint call with all the VCs. I wasn't very proud of the fact that I broke into tears during this call. 'Guys, what are you doing? The company will shut down. Please somehow save the company,' I pleaded, to no avail.

To say that I was disheartened would be an understatement. Not wanting to leave any stone unturned, I decided to call the super boss at VC One, since they had earlier made an offer of investment. 'I have taken a double bet on Flipkart. They are now entering the electronics space. I can't invest in two companies competing to make their mark in the same category. I could look at investing in LetsBuy, but that is if you agree to make a shift to some other category,' he said, explaining his rationale. 'Why don't you look at Williams Sonoma, and enter the home products segment?' he asked, by way of example. We were, however, too far entrenched in the electronics category to be able to make a quick pivot.

The happenings of the last few days had left LetsBuy in a very precarious position. At this time, we had money in the bank to last us around six months. If we had to take competitors like Flipkart head-on, it was a given that we would need a lot of capital.

It was a cold January morning that echoed the gloom in my own heart, when I finally convinced myself to make that phone call. With a beating heart, I reached out to the super boss at VC One to ask him if Flipkart would be open to acquiring the company. 'Let me think about it,' came his reply. I distinctly recall driving past Ambience Mall on the Gurgaon highway as my phone rang. It was him returning my call. He agreed to discuss the proposition with the Flipkart founders. After all, not only did we bring a lot of capability to the table, acquiring us would mean that they would have one less competitor to deal with. Subsequently he got Sachin and Binny Bansal of Flipkart to meet Hitesh and Aman, so they could all arrive at a decision.

'Flipkart has agreed,' VC One informed us over a call a few days later. It was the only confirmation we had received in some time. On the face of it, it was positive news, though a heartbreaking one. We could never have imagined, even a few days ago, that we would need to make a sale and how!

'Flipkart acquires Letsbuy.com' ran the headline in all dailies.

The deal went on to offer cash to the founders and equity to LetsBuy investors. Financially, the deal worked out well for all the founders and earlier investors but a big dream had crash-landed. In fact, while the founders settled for a small exit, the investors who converted their equity to Flipkart eventually must have made as much as fifteen to sixteen times on the deal. As for VCs Four, Five and Six, they received their money back and were in the clear. At our end, we took on the responsibility of winding down the company and worked very hard to take care of each employee who might face possible redundancy. Emotionally, of course, this wasn't the most desirable end to a journey that had started off on a promising note.

Several years later, as I sit down to think of this episode, I am left wondering what I could have done differently in the situation we were in. Maybe we shouldn't have agreed to go ahead with so many investors at the Series B stage; maybe we should have put our foot down when we had a hunch that the foreign company registration decision wasn't for us; maybe we should have taken more risk and pushed on, as opposed to settling for an exit. Above everything, maybe we should have listened to our inner voice a lot more.

But then hindsight is always known to be twenty/twenty.

Actionable Insights

Fundraising process: Much as a co-founder relationship is like a marriage, a relationship with investors is equally so. Investors in the company are a very important ingredient in the success of the company. They not only provide capital but also offer access to a network and are a great sounding board. Here are some points to consider in making the right choice of investor as also to do with the fundraising process:

Don't be overawed by investors: Investors are a very important part of the entrepreneur's success, no questions asked. While a lot of reference checks are done on founders, it's equally important that founders do some reference checks on investors. Most of the time founders don't have the luxury to do so because money coming into the company is considered more important than who is putting it in. However, it is best to choose wisely. Among other things a good investor–entrepreneur relationship requires that neither party abuse its power when it has an upper hand.

Fundraising is an art: Right from the time you get a term sheet to the time the money hits your bank, there are several aspects to be mindful of:

1. Ensure that you are prepared for the many rounds of due diligence that the company will be subject to. If you do not have experienced professionals internally to help execute them, make sure you hire one externally. Cutting costs to hire professional experts can turn out to be fatal.

2. Steer clear of premature announcements. While investors will claim that they never go back on their term sheets, it is best to take it with a pinch of salt. It isn't that they may deliberately choose to do so, industry environment or business metric changes may sometimes force them to do so. Engagement with the press, or anyone outside of founders in the team, must be avoided at the stage of the term sheet.

3. The fundraising process will completely absorb you as the founder. Ensure that you have trusted team members who keep a strong eye on growth, in the interim. Any negative performance at this time, more than ever, can hamper the fundraising process.

4. Deals are best when they are a win–win. It is prudent to therefore always leave something on the table.

Chapter 13

Business Card

'When God closes a door, He opens a window. — Old saying'

This oft-quoted adage was coming true for me in more ways than one. While LetsBuy, our e-commerce venture, had come to an untimely end, Tyroo, where I had taken over as the full-time founder CEO, was doing extremely well on the back of the growth of that very sector—e-commerce.

An ad tech platform, Tyroo brought together a number of publishers and allowed them to make their advertising inventory available to a wide range of clients that included banks, travel companies and now, increasingly, product e-commerce. In fact, thanks to my involvement in LetsBuy, I had got a first-hand perspective from a client's end and could add further value to the platform.

An Inspiration and a 'Cakey' Affirmation

Having taken over the operations at Tyroo, I was determined to scale it up; my ambition was that it should become the largest Indian digital media company. In all of this, a big inspiration for me was a media house—Network 18. Set up by Raghav Bahl, a serial entrepreneur, Network 18 was launched in 1993 and grew into one of the largest collections of media properties in India, before it was acquired by Reliance. Each time I met a Network 18 executive, I would make it a point to flip their business card and admire the sheer number of media brands the company owned, the logos of which occupied pride of place on the card. Collectively they were Network18 and each brand was responsible for its own vertical.

I had pinned one such card on the softboard in my office for it to work as a constant source of inspiration, determined as I was, to achieve a similar feat in the digital space. My vision for Tyroo was audacious—for it to become the first Indian digital media company to scale up to achieve revenues of Rs 100 crore from the current Rs 8 crore. Fortunately for me, I had an able team comprising Siddharth Puri and Ashwani Mehta. (On an aside, both Ashwani and Siddharth have had stellar journeys. Ashwani had joined Tyroo as a finance executive and is currently leading a digital media platform, while Siddharth Puri joined as a manager and is currently the co-founder of Tyroo). This duo not only supported me in my endeavours but also humoured me. In fact, every birthday that I celebrated at Tyroo had a similar cake, one that said, 'We will do 100 crores' by way of affirmation. This target aligned everyone to a common mission for Tyroo.

We had, by this time, bought back an additional stake in the company from Yahoo and were impatient to make a success out of Tyroo. At the core, I realized that even though we were positioned as a tech business, we were a services business, one that I wanted to grow and run profitably. I had already made it clear to the board that unless I had a clear direction, I wouldn't take on the task of fundraising even though we were staring at large funded competitors. In fact, I also made sure that we didn't burn the funds that we had raised earlier from Yahoo. My philosophy was that a large part of the funds raised should be kept away as rainy-day capital or for interesting opportunities that might present themselves. While most companies do not work on this philosophy, I ensured that we had a sizable amount of capital as reserve while attempting to build profitability and scale. We coined the term 'profitable growth' in the services business while most of the industry played only for 'growth'. Fortunately for me, while there was pressure in terms of fundraising, Harish was fully aligned with this thought and the board had faith in my abilities. Therefore, I had a free hand in building the company. What also worked for me was the fact that there was a tailwind in the market that we could take advantage of.

Scaling Up on the Back of an Insight

An important insight that I acquired at the time was that if advertisers were willing to part with Rs 1000 on Google or Facebook to acquire a customer, the corresponding amount that they were willing to pay on most Indian performance media networks, including Tyroo, was only Rs 300. I was quite taken aback at this startling difference, considering that the customer profile that Tyroo offered was similar. While

I raised my concerns with Siddharth, I reasoned that this was on account of our pricing. 'Let us raise our pricing by 3X and we will automatically be at 3X of our revenue,' I said to him. 'Yes, but advertisers will not be willing to pay that price,' came his reply. That led me to the core problem—the fact that the issue lay in our positioning. So far, we were positioned as a performance media network (that is typically perceived to be the lowest in the hierarchy). This led to the perception that the quality of customers that we offered was poor. Advertisers were using us as a price averaging bucket. We clearly needed to change our positioning to a customer acquisition engine (CAE), from that of a performance media network, for advertisers to realize that the quality of customers that we were offering was at par. That led to a sea change in all our pitches. It instilled a different energy into our business and the numbers slowly started showing an upward climb.

For three straight years, we showed impressive YoY growth riding on this strategy, building our corpus in the process. Siddharth, all this while, was playing on the front foot, turning out to be an able executing partner. My collaboration with Siddharth, in fact, reminded me of the strong bond Harish and I had built when we had begun our entrepreneurial journey together. Of course, having spent several years working with Harish, I looked up to him as more than a partner—I saw him as a friend and an elder brother. Among other things, I could never forget that it was Harish, along with my father, who had a strong role to play in keeping me on the entrepreneurial path when I had nearly succumbed to the temptation of a plum job at Google.

Network 18 Dream

'Would you like to buy DGM india?'

I was in Malaysia for a holiday when I received a call from Mr Swaroop, who posed this question to me. By this time, Mr Swaroop had sold his equity in Tyroo but had stayed in touch. It was Mr Swaroop's old colleague, Anurag Gupta, who had reached out to him with the proposition of acquiring the India arm of the global affiliate network called DGM. Apparently, its India division had run into some financial difficulties, prompting Gupta to get in touch with Mr Swaroop, asking if Tyroo would be interested in a potential buyout.

My instant reply to Mr Swaroop's question was 'Let's look into it.' The one thing I had learnt in my journey as an entrepreneur was that curiosity and hustling were two muscles that had always stood me in good stead. I earnestly believed in the adage, 'Never say never'. It was this sense of positive opportunism that I showed at every step, big or small, that I believed had led me to where I was. As an example, when we were looking at an office space with a budget of Rs 7–10 crore and the broker wanted to show me a particularly exciting space that cost Rs 40 crore, far beyond our reach, I didn't say no to seeing the space. Who knew that the space, while being unaffordable then, would become the inspiration we needed to scale the next milestone?

It was with this mindset that I agreed to meet Anurag Gupta. A meeting held at Mr Swaroop's home, on my return, saw us exploring the possibility of buying out DGM's India arm. I asked Anurag to front the deal while we participated in it. I was very excited at the thought that if the deal truly came through, this would be Tyroo's first ever acquisition.

'The deal isn't working out at the price that you had indicated,' I was informed by Anurag several days later, much to my disappointment. This, however, prompted me to act proactively and reach out to the DGM founder, Adrian. While he lived out of China, Singapore and London, we arranged for a meeting to be held in Singapore. To cut a long story short, Adrian's ask was way above what we could commit to from our cash reserves. I was reluctant to let the deal go. On discussing the issue with Harish, the two of us jointly agreed to slightly increase our offer, convinced of the value that DGM would bring to the table.

A second meeting with Adrian, with a revised offer, turned out to be the clincher. The reserves that we had kept aside from the Yahoo investment, as also the corpus that we had built in the intervening years came in handy. We had made our first acquisition. The Network 18 business card, as I had envisaged it for Tyroo, was beginning to fill up.

Actionable Insights

Creating reciprocal advantage:

Running a successful business involves putting together some very important pieces, primary among them being:

The right team: While I spoke of the team members sharing a common vision earlier, some of the other aspects that help build a great team include looking for people who have:

Compatibility quotient (CQ): Are team members compatible with the style of the leadership and its cultural aspect?

Time quotient (TQ): Do team members reflect longevity in their style of association or are they hoppers from company to company?

Reward quotient (RQ): Are team members a 'reward to action' personalities, i.e., can a 20 per cent additional compensation from a competitor sway them away or are they hungry to stay, learn and grow?

Upskilling quotient (UQ): Are team members elastic and open to upskilling themselves in terms of new business responsibilities and skills?

This is not to say that all expectations need to rest with the team. The leader has a stronger mantle to carry as he or she needs to:

- Create a supportive and inclusive environment where individuals can thrive and grow. Start-up stories are replete with the incidence of toxic work cultures. It is a self-defeating cycle. Unless individuals can thrive and reach their full potential, there is no way a business can.

- Have a distributed leadership framework. Concentrated leadership at the top is a recipe for politics and high dependence.

- Employees need to make wealth just as founders do. ESOP buybacks, for one, need to come before or at least together with the founder's secondary sale.

- Early on, avoid making someone 'head' because it creates entitlement. Optimize for hands on builders and not titles

Knowledge drives wealth: 'Saraswati ji will drive Lakshmi ji' (Goddess of Knowledge will drive Goddess of Wealth), Harish has always maintained. This is the age of the knowledge economy. You have to find ways to continuously upskill yourself as well as your team.

You don't own the business: I have always believed that as a founder, you do not own a business. It is the business entity that has appointed you to run it. The shareholder of a business, when working in an executive capacity, should see himself or herself as the sevak of the business and its customers. It's nothing more than a responsibility bestowed on them.

Chapter 14

Flying High

A new name.

Over the next few days, Harish and I scouted for a name for a holding company (holdco) that we needed to incorporate, now that we had two companies under our umbrella, Tyroo and DGM.

During the period in which Harish and I had gone our separate ways with our e-commerce ventures, I had formulated a company for my holdings called Vaana Ventures (Vaana meaning forest in Hindi). All our companies, and others, were already operating under Smile Group—that Harish founded. The idea for the name of our holdco came from combining these two names—we decided to call ourselves SVG Media. It was decided that I would function as the CEO of the holdco, with Ashwani assisting me for the finance function, while Tyroo would be run by Siddharth Puri and DGM by Anurag Gupta, both as the business heads and CEOs of their respective businesses. Anurag, an IIM-A alumnus, was a veteran in the digital affiliate Industry. (Unfortunately, we lost him in 2019 at a young age). Together we are all on a mission of delivering unmatched digital performance marketing to Indian internet companies.

A Sale and More Acquisitions

There are seventy-eight organs in our body. Ever since the mobile phone made its entrance into the market, however, it has nearly become an intrinsic body part, taking the number of organs seemingly up to seventy-nine. It was with this thought that, when I incubated a mobile media company, I decided to name it SeventyNine. The company was run by Deven, a close friend and a founding team member of Quasar, and Chirag Shah as co-founders. Deven had, by this time, completed his commitments at WPP (as part of Quasar's exit to WPP) and was looking forward to working with me again.

It so happened that around the time SVG Media was formed, I received an offer from a gentleman called Ram Mohan Sundaram, a well-regarded digital media entrepreneur in India, who was Founder and CEO of a company called NetworkPlay, which had been acquired by Gruner + Jahr, a media company, which is a part of Germany's Bertelsmann group. They were interested in acquiring SeventyNine. One of the reasons I considered exiting SeventyNine was to be able to consolidate all digital media operations under SVG Media (of which Tyroo and DGM were now a part). We ended up selling SeventyNine to Bertelsmann. Fate, however, had other plans.

Around a year after SeventyNine was sold, I heard from Deven. 'Gruner + Jahr has decided to exit the country,' he said animatedly. 'How about a buy back along with the management?' he asked me, rubbing his excitement onto me.

It so happened that we were able to acquire not just SeventyNine but also NetworkPlay. The clincher was that the acquisition of both these companies came at a cost lower than the one at which we had sold SeventyNine.

The Network 18 business card that I had stuck at my work desk as inspiration was clearly coming in handy. SVG Media now had four logos to showcase, Tyroo, DGM, NetworkPlay and SeventyNine.

'*Yaar, Manish, kamaal ho gaya* (Manish, this is amazing),' I patted my back on this milestone. In about three years of operations, Tyroo was already at Rs 100 crore of revenue that we had envisaged, while we now also had three other brands in our kitty. We were clearly on a dream run and even had a global footprint, having set up offices in China, the Middle East and Singapore. What added to the entire experience was a dream team, a supportive partner and an equally supportive board.

An Unlikely Acquisition

At this time, the right thing for me to do for SVG was to expand its footprint. One company I always had an eye on was Komli Media. Founded by Amar Goel, Komli's India business offered cross-device solutions across social media and video for marketers and publishers, and would have been a great addition to the SVG stable.

Komli enjoyed a great brand name and had an exceptional founding team. I knew, however, that while the company had raised several funding rounds, amounting to double digit millions and counted some large names as its investors, it wasn't profitable and was facing issues in raising more funds. In such a situation, investors can write you off as a line item in their Excel sheet, but for a founder, since you are the whole Excel sheet, the stakes are very high. I instinctively knew that its founders must be under pressure.

At an ad tech event when I saw Amar Goel, the co-founder of Komli, I decided to reach out to him directly. The acquisitions that we had made in the intervening years had filled me with a certain confidence to be able to approach these issues head on. 'Do let me know if you would like to explore any opportunity for a strategic partnership,' I remember telling Amar at the end of a casual conversation, without even knowing if he was indeed looking for one. It turned out that my hunch was correct, for the very next day, I received a call from him to tell me that they were looking at exiting the space and that he would be open to receiving an offer from me. While I had done well to sniff out an opportunity, the fact remained that we had limited reserves. Nonetheless, driven by my curiosity and the never-say-never approach, I decided to give the deal a shot.

The first thing that I did was to buy time, since I did not want to come across as being overly keen. I also used this time to speak to ex-Komli folks, who confirmed that the company had an asset that could be revived. One month into our initial conversation, I received a call from Amar. 'Do let me know if you have anything in mind,' he asked. 'I have an offer but you may feel embarrassed if I share it. Let's meet and chat,' I replied. Amar invited me to come down to their Mumbai office to discuss things in detail. This time I decided to play on the front foot, and be totally honest about the funds we had at hand. Besides, I knew that there weren't any other offers on the table for Komli. 'I have a limited amount in our company's bank account,' I said upfront, to Amar's initial shock. 'I am happy to give all of it to you,' I continued, undeterred. What I had done was not to undermine their brand value, but to place my cards on the table, upfront. Perhaps that is what led Amar to say yes.

'*SVG acquires Komli Media's India business*,' ran the headlines in all the business dailies. We were once again in the news, for all the right reasons. The press coverage highlighted the fact that SVG was well poised to deliver a comprehensive suite of digital marketing products. On our part, we reiterated that we were working hard to be the leading Asian digital marketing platform from India. This further positioned SVG Media as a strong player. The fantastic team of leaders that included Siddharth Puri, Deven Dharamdasani, Chirag Shah, Ashwani Mehta, Anurag Gupta and Akshay Mathur were my partners and stars. We were a force in the Indian digital media scene.

Needless to say, Komli's acquisition filled me with a lot of confidence.

By this time, we were the largest Indian digital media network by a huge margin and the third largest digital media company, in India, after Google and Facebook, and we were profitable.

We had already set our sights on the next milestone. It was time to go public.

Actionable Insights

Growth strategy aligned to your business model:

There are broadly two types of businesses:

- Winners-take-it-all businesses (Category A): These are category disruptors and play on low margin but high-volume e.g e-commerce / retail.
- Multiple winner businesses (Category B): These are well established businesses with high margins and a very large market for multiple players to be able to scale e.g services.

I, for one, have been part of building both kind of businesses. Category A businesses require a lot of capital for a long time to be able to disrupt the market and create strong entry barriers. In such businesses, founders need to be confident of their fundraising skills to be able to ensure a constant supply of capital, besides having a strong focus on micro level financial discipline and operational excellence. These companies do get trapped chasing capital and growth. However, even here undisciplined growth is a tactic and not a strategy.

Category B businesses, on the other hand, need to focus on 'profitable growth'. These businesses can be bootstrapped or built through fund raising. In both cases it is best to keep a strong focus on unit level profitability and invest every penny of the profit earned towards gaining higher market share. Market share and leadership is also important in category B businesses since the value of the business lies in being the leader or at least a close number 2.

Chapter 15

Bittersweet

Rs 300 crore: that was the revenue that SVG Media had clocked in 2016. The acquisition of Komli Media had turned out to be an asset. Fortunately for me, Akshay Mathur, one of the old hands at Komli, decided to stay on and lead the company. With his inputs and all our tireless efforts, we were able to turn the company around to make it super profitable.

'Let us start talking to bankers to give shape to our IPO dream,' Harish and I discussed, wanting the company to take a new leap. Conversations with several banks followed. If we were holding these conversations about going public in today's milieu with similar growth patterns, we would certainly be valued at about a billion dollars, given the Indian market's appetite for tech stocks now. Nearly a decade ago however, the popular opinion of bankers, regarding a company of our size, wasn't so strong.

Having made up our minds to go the IPO route, we felt that the best way forward was to acquire other companies in the space, in order for us to hit a bigger number. I reached out to several companies that had a strong synergy with us. The pitch that I made to each of them had a common theme. 'Let us together build a formidable digital media company in India, one that Google and Facebook cannot think of guzzling up,'

I said. By and large, however, each conversation boiled down to the fact that entrepreneurial ego in founder colleagues did not allow them to sell their business to us. We also needed larger reserves in the company for bigger acquisitions.

'If the IPO isn't happening in India, let's explore other markets,' we discussed, confident that if the time wasn't ripe for an Indian IPO, we could still look at other avenues. While NASDAQ was a distant dream, our first port of call was Singapore. Research, however, led us to the fact that the Singapore Exchange wasn't the best listing option when it came to liquidity. We were then led by experts to explore the Australian Stock Exchange. Not only did Harish and I make several trips to Australia, we even hired Macquarie Bank to do the groundwork for us.

A Chance Meeting

Around the time that I was feverishly trying to give life to our IPO dream, Anurag Gupta, my partner and leader of DGM, wanted to explore strategic exit opportunities. An IPO typically meant that everyone had to be on a constant treadmill. Gupta, eight years my senior, did not envision that kind of a future for himself and thought that an exit would work well for him.

I mentioned the potential sale of DGM to a friend, Vivek Bhargava, at a chance meeting at the Four Seasons Hotel in Mumbai. Bhargava was the founder of Communicate2, a media company that had recently been acquired by Dentsu Aegis Network, a large media and digital marketing communications company headquartered in London. While he heard me out, his sudden, follow-up question took me by surprise. 'Would you consider selling SVG?' Bhargava asked me, led by the fact that Dentsu was currently on an acquisition spree. My answer, of course, was an emphatic no. 'Selling is not in our plans. We are looking at going the IPO route,' I said to him intuitively.

We were enjoying a snug winter lunch that I had hosted at my home in Gurgaon's DLF, where I had invited the heads of all the business units of SVG along with their families, when I mentioned the meeting with Vivek Bhargava. 'Out of the blue, Bhargava mentioned that Dentsu could be interested in buying out SVG. It took me by surprise and I told him that we weren't planning to go that route at all,' I recounted. If I thought everyone else would be equally surprised at the near absurdity of the suggestion, I was in for a surprise myself. Instead of summarily dismissing the idea, it led to a long discussion on the merits of selling the company vis-a-vis going the IPO route. Several of the business heads felt that going in for an IPO was a long journey that involved back-breaking work. They were of the opinion that if we received a real offer from Dentsu, it would be worth considering. Harish and I quietly absorbed the discussion. Looking back, I believe that the entire conversation was driven by individual aspirations as well as personal fatigue levels, as opposed to the best way forward for the business entity. In hindsight, I realize how we give the passengers and driver of the car (read: business entity) more weightage than the car itself, when it is the car that needs to be kept above individual goals and aspirations. At this point, since we didn't have any firm offer from Dentsu in hand, it was decided that while we would continue to work on the IPO plan, we could also explore this idea by the side. Once again, in hindsight, that turned out to be a mistake. For when you don't intend to take a particular path, it is best to nip any thoughts of it in the bud.

While we had decided to explore both paths parallely, there were two big realizations we came to in the coming days. The first, that the offer that Dentsu could make was nearly as large as the money that would be involved in the IPO. Secondly, while the IPO was a long-winded, slow process, the discussions with Dentsu seemed to catapult quite fast, once we had taken the first step.

Each time that the issue came up for discussion internally, everyone seemed to be that much more tilted to the side where there were immediate gains. To put it simply, popular opinion seemed to be that we should consider jumping off the entrepreneurial treadmill for now, take the fairly large amount of money on offer and, at an opportune time, get around to building something else. The point that we were missing was that the momentum that a business entity builds is a function of a number of factors that come together .Its people, brands, processes, the cash flow and a lot more form a winning combination that isn't easy to replicate. Essentially, while we were tilting towards a decision where individuals gained, it was also a decision where the platform that we had built would lose.

Personally, I was inclined towards taking the IPO route and was also confident that if I made the decision, I would receive the support of the team. One big hurdle in the IPO route, in India, however, was the fact that we needed to acquire an equally large company so that we could reach a desired revenue to attract high quality investors for a successful listing. I decided to speak with one such competitor, a digital media platform run by very respected founders. Reaching out to its co-founder, I emphasized the fact that this was our big chance to create a large company and go public jointly. While they liked the idea conceptually, they were more inclined towards listing on the Singapore exchange, by themselves. This was an option that we had already explored and turned down on account of issues of liquidity. I even shared with the co-founders the fact that we had an offer on the table and that if they agreed to our proposal, we would turn it down and together build history. The co-founder of that business, however, felt that he needed time and couldn't act on it immediately.

All this time, I had been resisting the Dentsu offer. I was now forced to sit down and give it some serious thought. To be fair, thoughts of how the money could change the lives of everyone involved and also catapult me from an upper middle-class experience towards a high-net-worth individual (HNI), seemed to take centre stage. In all of this, I was convincing myself that if I made the sale, I could always put my energies behind building yet another platform. Consumed by these thoughts, I finally ended up giving my consent to the offer.

D-Day

'I need an hour to step out and get some fresh air into my system,' I said as we all sat in Mumbai on the appointed day of signing the sale document. The emotional aspect of selling a company that we had built so painstakingly and that had so much going for itself was still weighing upon me. In this one hour that I took out for myself, my entire life seemed to flash in front of my eyes. I recalled how my entrepreneurial journey had begun with KabadiBazaar and how heartbroken I had been when the global crash led to its untimely end. I remembered how we had taken the first few quivering steps towards the launch of Quasar, emboldened by the encouragement of well-meaning friends who had advised me to find my escape velocity. The incidents that led to the launch of Tyroo, Quasar's subsequent JV with WPP, the LetsBuy journey and its eventual sale to Flipkart, the launch of SVG and the many companies that found pride of place on its business card, flashed in my memory. Trying to come to terms with the decision we had now committed ourselves to, I penned down an email to all the partners, their wives and my co-founder who had played an intrinsic role in the building of SVG. The one thing I firmly believed in and that I acknowledged in the mail was that 'Success is a combination of many destinies coming together.' I was certain that it wasn't just my destiny that had led this starry-eyed boy, who had started out with yarn trading from a PCO, to be selling a company for millions of dollars.

'Dentsu Aegis acquires SVG Media in all-cash deal'

'This marks the second successful exit by Vij and Bahl in the digital media space, after having sold ad firm Quasar Media to WPP Digital in 2007. Separately, LetsBuy, an electronics retail venture e-commerce platform set up by Vij, was sold to Flipkart in 2012.'

The front page of all the business dailies carried this news. It was truly a bittersweet moment, one that had brought huge financial gains to us but that was also heart-wrenching at the same time.

The SVG sale agreement gave Harish and me a clear exit while most business heads stood to earn a substantial amount over a three-year earnout. The sale also ensured a ten times greater return for our investors. Amidst all these bullish stories of financial gain, if there was one story that really tugged at my heartstrings, it was that of a peon at SVG who, having been allocated ESOPs at the time of the launch, now stood to earn as much as Rs 5 lakh, an amount that was life-changing for him. The gratitude and happiness in his eyes, as he came up to thank us, felt like my biggest entrepreneurial earning at the time.

Another heartening aspect of the sale was that while Dentsu acquired all of SVG, it didn't have any interest in Tyroo, it being a tech company. That meant that we could still keep Tyroo and retain a foothold in the media space. In fact, Siddharth Puri, who had operationally run Tyroo during this period, became its co-founder and also invested part of the exit proceeds as a show of confidence.

When Harish and I opened a bottle of champagne on my thirty-ninth birthday that year, it wasn't only to mark the successful end to our entrepreneurial run, but also to celebrate a new partnership, one that would not just build businesses but assist young people to realize their entrepreneurial dreams.

Actionable Insights

Keeping entrepreneurial fatigue at bay:

While we are often awed by headlines about multi-million-dollar fundings, business exits, start-ups achieving unicorn status and more, not many of us realize that entrepreneurship is in effect a long, arduous journey. Many have described it as being constantly on the treadmill. Building sustainable good businesses are at least 15 years+ journeys and founder and leadership fatigue is a reality. Some of the things that can help in the journey include:

- Work–life harmony: For too long, we have lived with the notion that work and life exist as separate, opposing entities and that we need to strike a balance between the two. The process is exhausting, especially since the pursuit of 'balance' implies a perfect equilibrium where any movement could tip the scales. With creativity and intention, we need to work towards work-life harmony—where you craft a lifestyle that allows you to thrive in all the facets of your life. As Sheryl Sandberg, former COO of Meta, says, 'Bring your whole self to work. I don't believe we have a professional self Monday through Friday and a real self the rest of the time. It is all professional and it is all personal.'

- Finding time for breaks: Taking the road less travelled is hard, lonely and stressful. There are moments of great highs, terrible lows and unrelenting stress. Picking a hobby that you love is therefore not just nice-to-have but a must have. As my respected uncle and guru ji says 'One should try to become a kid for an hour everyday'. Some things that have worked for me are travel (short, long and adventurous) and spending time with family and friends.

Chapter 16

Pay It Forward

Let us take a seven-day trip driving through the cities of Jordan.

That was my text message to the senior leadership team at SVG, following its sale to Dentsu. While the SVG journey had come to an end, the teamwork and the camaraderie we had built there went far beyond the realms of a company, of the profits we had earned, and more. It was to celebrate this eventful journey that Harish and I decided to go with our erstwhile team for a trip that would help us recall old times and build new memories. The seven-day trip where we drove through the cities of Jordan, charting new horizons as well as reminiscing about the time and learnings that we had shared remains fresh in all our memories.

Back home, Harish and I spent a lot of time discussing what we wanted to do next. While retiring at forty is a dream that many of us harbour, I was certain that if God had given me so much, I needed to think of ways to pay it forward.

Typically, following an exit, entrepreneurs are faced with three paths—start up once again, set up a family office and manage wealth or turn into a venture capitalist. By the process of elimination, I knew that simply managing wealth or turning into a VC wasn't for me. Having spent long years as an entrepreneur, being close to where the action was, was second nature to me. I couldn't trade that for a sedentary life. At this time Harish came up with a suggestion that made me sit up and think. 'Why don't you come along and partner me in Smile, for venture building entrepreneurs wherein we don't just invest in their business but also play a strong role in helping build their business?' Harish's leadership and vision towards building Smile and its companies as a leading digital group was in any case truly remarkable and a tale worth telling in its own right. When we now started discussing the venture build idea together, it started coming to life for me. I had always believed that the soul of a start-up is its founder. As long as we could partner with passionate early-stage founders who lived and breathed their business and could offer them a strong support system, we could fulfil our twin objective of paying it forward as well as staying close to the action, as entrepreneurs.

Tyroo, carved out of SVG Media's sale to Dentsu, became our first venture build together. Siddharth Puri invested a part of his gains from the SVG media exit to become its shareholder and co-founder. The core team of Vaibhav Gupta and Akshay Mathur continued to be part of Tyroo's leadership. Today, Tyroo is on a mission to build an APAC focused market entry and growth platform for global media and tech businesses.

A Visit to a Temple and an Idea

I was on a road trip in Rajasthan when we decided to stop by at Shrinathji Mandir, Nathdwara, located about 50 kilometres away from Udaipur. The temple was shut at that time of the day and there was a huge crowd waiting for the doors to be opened.

While we stood in the serpentine queue, I noticed that most people were playing games on their smartphones. In fact, if there was one thing that cut through the varying demographics and social status of the people, besides their devotion, it had to be the games they were playing. It was like a moment of truth for me and I realized that gaming was be a sector that we needed to look at. I discussed this opportunity with Harish and he was excited too.

I attended various gaming events and conferences to get a fair idea of the segment. What I realized in the process was that monetization in the gaming business in India could not come from advertising revenue. We clearly had to look at a transactional pay-to-play model. Prior to doing that, I wanted to understand the legal ramifications of the model, which led me to Vidushpat Singhania, a leading lawyer who specialized in gaming and entertainment laws. Duly convinced by him that this was a creditable sector to look at, I now began my search for an early-stage entrepreneur who was already working in this domain and was passionate to make it big. It was once again hustle and serendipity that led me to meet the co-founders of Zupee.

Dilsher Malhi, and his co-founder Siddhant Saurabh, both graduates from IIT–Kanpur, had the kind of spark we were looking for. Zupee went on to become our first venture build company under our partnership. With Dilsher and Siddhant working from our office, and with us backing them as their first

investors and venture-building partners, the energy was electric.
The first game that Zupee developed was a quiz game that soon
became the largest in the country. Zupee subsequently went on
to receive its Series A funding from Matrix Partners and Series
B from WestCap and other reputed investors. Emboldened by
this ratification, we put our energies behind developing other
skill-based games that were culturally popular. Today, Zupee
is one of the leading gaming companies in India, led by its
founder Dilsher Malhi, one that we take great pride in.

Otipy

On a trip to Goa, I said to Harish, 'I would love to do
something wherein we use the digital medium to help people
earn—something like social commerce.'

'Why don't we look at setting up something that makes
fresh farm produce available to consumers directly—a model
that has shown success in China?' came Harish's suggestion.
That led to the idea of building a social commerce venture
that would enable consumers to receive fresh farm food while
also ensuring that farmers receive a fair price for their produce.
From the business perspective, unlike e-commerce, we wouldn't
have to struggle with a high customer acquisition cost. It was
therefore a win–win situation for all. With this idea, we reached
out to Varun Khurana who ran an agri-tech start-up, Crofarm.
We pitched this idea to him and he was excited to invite us

as his early investor partner and pivot Crofarm to a social commerce business.

This gave rise to the birth of Otipy, our next venture build company. Today the company services as many as 30,000 orders a day, ensuring that fresh farm produce is made available to homes. A Covid baby, Otipy is now a successful company past its Series B from marquee investors.

Overall, the journey of the past few years, alongside a world-class team that includes Ramit and others, has been extremely fulfilling as we continue to partner founders who have an insatiable desire to solve challenges. We are truly living Smile's mission of 'founders scaling founders'.

Picture Abhi Baaki Hai

The itch to solve problems and build businesses keeps me going. Who knows where my journey will lead me. The only thing that I know for sure is that several dots joined together to bring me to a position where I could make a small difference in the business world.

Main kisi ke lagaye hue paed ke phal kha raha hoon, isliye mujhe aur paed lagane se peeche nahi hatna hai (I am enjoying the fruit of trees planted by others, and I have to continue to pay forward and keep planting trees myself)! Having shared my story with you it is time for me to get back to work.

Actionable Insights

Make your 'strong the strongest': It takes time for the business or an individual, to build an area of super strength, a strong moat, and find its feet. Once you find your 'strong' this is the time to continuously make 'your strong the strongest'. This is not something that is easily achieved by all businesses. Therefore, if and when you achieve it, you need to strive for being the best-in-class.

Aagey badhte raho **(keep moving forward):** Making unprofitable business decisions, forging unfruitful partnerships, hiring the wrong leadership, saying yes to a bad deal, missing very big business opportunities, etc, have all been part and parcel of my journey. You will go through your own set of mistakes. Through all this, you need to be kind to yourself and keep a positive attitude. I, for one, recall having lost approximately ~40 per cent of the personal wealth that we made through an acquisition, in a matter of months, in investing in the stock market. I also made the mistake of inadvertently issuing equity shares to a team member, instead of ESOPs, without seeking the concurrence of the Board. While these decisions are regrettable, beyond a point you cannot sit and rue your decisions. You have to cut your losses and carry on in the spirit of having learnt important lessons from the failure. Think of entrepreneurial life like a stream that will flow, irrespective of the rocks in between.

Pay it forward: Statistics show that as many as nine out of ten start-ups fail. If you are among the successful ones, then a lot has worked for your business. Product, team, timing, your hard work . . . everything has come together. Now go ahead and pay things forward. As poet Maya Angelou put it, 'You shouldn't go through life with a catcher's mitt on both hands. You need to be able to throw something back.'

Epilogue

While you know the highlights of my entrepreneurial journey by now, I firmly believe that my real learning as well as earning has been the lives that I could impact. In parting, beyond the entrepreneurial insights, I would like to leave you with some life lessons that I have amassed during my journey. Should any of these resonate with you or help you in any aspect of your life, I will achieve the objective with which I took to writing this book. For, as one of my favourite quotes goes, we are all just walking each other home.

'Serendipity is the universe's way of saying; I've got your back': There can be no bigger learning for me than the fact that you need to trust the universe. If I look back, it will be hard not to notice how so many dots joined to get me to the place I am at today. From landing up in Indore for a course that I had no idea about, to taking to entrepreneurship purely as a means to find a job, little knowing that it would become my life's calling, there are serendipitous events strewn all through my life's journey. The people that I met along the way, right from my first boss who coaxed me to resign from my job to pursue entrepreneurship, to colleagues and mentors who urged me to find my 'escape velocity', there is a role that each of them were destined to play. In fact, each time I set out with the maxim of *aage badhte hain, dekha jayega* (keep moving, things will fall into place) and have taken well-meaning steps, a safety net has appeared. My landing at the doorstep of a renowned lawyer, for instance, armed with nothing but a belief that the universe will rise to my rescue, led me to meet this kind gentleman who took up my case and fought it pro bono. Put on your logical hat and you cannot even imagine something so bizarre. If you look at the businesses I have been part of as founder / co-founder, an ongoing business partnership of 20+ years and the funding rounds that these businesses have raised, for instance, you cannot deny the fact that I was at the right place at the right time. From starting out with an audacious idea to turning into a poster boy in digital media circles and then investing in successful start-ups—can any of this be called anything short of miraculous? If I had to give one life changing advice to anyone, it would be to allow serendipity to become your co-pilot. You will not be disappointed.

All of this is not to say that you need to be fatalistic and not put your best foot forward to execute relentlessly. If success is in surrender, it is also in building the muscles of curiosity and hustling, a fact that I have emphasized throughout the book. Isn't that a dichotomy, you ask? Not quite, if you hear this example, that a *Granthi* (a ceremonial reader of the Guru Granth Sahib) once quoted to me. He recounted that in olden times, when people lived in houses with *aangans* or courtyards, they would often put their utensils out there. These utensils could either be kept face up or face down. When it rained, the utensils that were kept face up collected the rainwater. In the context of life, he explained, it is only when you are that *khula bartan*, the utensil kept face up, that you will be a receptacle of God's mercies. You don't know when it will rain or how much, but you need to prepare yourself so that when it does rain, you make the most of it. In short, serendipity will strike, but you have to respect it with humility and be in the driver's seat to take advantage of it, when it does. That, to my mind, pretty much explains the seeming dichotomy between fate and free will.

The power of belief and blessings: As a family, we are associated with Ram Sharnam Ashram in Gohana and Panipat. Our frequent visits and the opportunity to sit personally with our guru (and my family elders) to hear their wisdom have been a source of immense blessings. In fact, I am certain that it is the blessings that I have amassed along my journey that have helped me, even when I thought that it was my own efforts bearing fruit.

While most of us see blessings as a reward for productivity, I have learnt that it is what powers productivity. Let me offer an example. I grew up as a fairly average student. Despite my lack of academic success, my mother and my grandmother, in particular, went about telling me and everyone else who would care to listen, *'Manish bahot bada aadmi banega* (Manish will grow up to be very successful).' Subconsciously, I believe it was their intrinsic faith in me that gave me the power to live up to their dreams.

I remember how my father told me a story of a man spending the night in a freezing pond on a winter's night. On being asked the next morning how he had achieved this impossible feat, he recounted that he had spotted a small flame burning in the distance that had given him hope and kept him going. In my case, this flame was my mother's and grandmother's appreciation and belief in me. Parents, I believe, have a very important role to play in bringing up children, believing in their inherent abilities and helping them build self-esteem in the process. I was blessed with caring parents.

In fact, not just my parents, but also my brother, Harshit, who is the founder of freecultr.com, has stood as solid as a rock, supporting me in all my endeavours. My wife has been yet another strong pillar of support in my entrepreneurial journey. She has never asked how much I earn but instead has encouraged me to take calculated risks with new business opportunities. As a family, we have gone through some very tough times, (well that's for another book), and each time my mother and wife have stood tall, and have supported me. My mother, specifically, has been through very challenging times in terms of her health and otherwise but each time she has acted with a lot of strength, managing the family. Today I derive a lot of my strength from our family—my parents, my wife Tina, my two beautiful teens, Vrinda and Viraj, my brother Harshit, his wife Akanksha, and their daughter, the youngest member of our family, Shrija.

You are the average of the five people you spend the most time with: I would like to increase the ambit of this oft-quoted saying. I believe that the more people you meet and the diverse experiences you gather, your perspective on life takes on a whole new meaning. I, for one, have benefited extremely from my adventure travels and from meeting hitherto unknown people. Whether it was being a part of the first Indian contingent who drove on the Icelandic glaciers (and creating a record in the Limca Book of Records) or driving in the Rocky Mountains in Canada and the deserts of Jordan—each of these experiences have taught me far more than anything I could have learnt either in classrooms or boardrooms. My half-marathons and weekly short runs have been a continuous source of strength for me. In fact, if you indulge me just a wee bit more, I would like to share a life-changing experience that happened to me, once again serendipitously. A few years ago, I was approached by Utkarsh Mishra, someone I didn't know, with a request for a sponsorship for a trip to Antarctica. On asking for the details, I found out that the trip was being organized by Robert Swan, the famous British explorer and global environmental activist who became the first person to successfully walk to both the South Pole and the North Pole. Swan is an advocate for the protection of the climate in general, and Antarctica in particular, and the founder of 2041, a foundation which is dedicated to the preservation of Antarctica through the promotion of environmental education, particularly among young people. His foundation has organized several public expeditions to Antarctica, to inspire and educate future environmental leaders. Utkarsh, the person that I was introduced to, was aspiring to go on one such expedition. Deeply intrigued by the work Swan was undertaking, I wanted to get on to this expedition myself. With applications closing and the time required for getting a visa being limited, once again the universe conspired to let me in on this life changing journey. After a whopping fifty-six hours of travel from New Delhi to London, to New York and onwards to Rio De Janeiro and Buenos Aires, we finally landed in the Argentinian city of Ushuaia, quite literally the Kanya Kumari of the earth, from where the nine-day voyage by ship was to begin. It was here that I met 100 unknown people who would be going on this voyage with me, with a common purpose. A big hurdle still remained; should any one test positive for the dreaded Covid-19 virus, the dream of being on that ship would end. Even aboard the ship, Covid tests were undertaken every single day with anyone testing positive being put into a basement bunker. Through all this, the ship made its way through the Drake Passage, a body of water between South America's Cape Horn, Chile, Argentina and the South Shetland Islands of Antarctica, which is considered one of the most treacherous voyages with waves topping as much as 40 feet.

The nine days spent aboard that ship were life-changing, to say the least. A big moment of truth for me was when all of us first started to introduce ourselves to each other. I realized how the wealth that any of us had amassed seemed so inconsequential, compared to the far-reaching impact on lives that some of us had created.

If there is one thing that I would recommend to everyone, it is to travel as much as possible; it opens your eyes to perspectives that you would otherwise miss. A fellow traveller on board this ship, a young professional who was just starting out on his career, shared with me how he wanted to amass experiences, and not possessions. That is a thought that has stayed with me.

Transformation of lives is your biggest reward: I have mentioned this in passing before but it deserves to be listed as a life lesson. The biggest earnout that I have received in my journey is not the companies we have built or the personal wealth that we all have made, but the lives that I have had the good fortune of impacting. I take immense pride in the fact that members of the team of Quasar/LetsBuy/SVG/Smile are today entrepreneurs in their own right, running large and successful start-ups, delivering impact and employing hundreds. I believe we would have directly or indirectly influenced over a hundred entrepreneurs in India. Each time we meet, not only do they fondly recall our time together but also the fact that the learning acquired then came in extremely handy on their own journeys. Just the other day, I met an ex-employee of SVG who invited me to his home, one that he had been able to build with the ESOPs he had earned. The story of the peon's life being transformed as he became debt-free is extremely close to my heart, one that I have recounted before.

I say all of this with great humility as I believe I have been extremely fortunate to have been blessed to be a medium for all of this. There were many people who helped me on my journey selflessly. All I can do is to pay it forward.

Acknowledgements

Many people have played an integral role in my life and entrepreneurial journey. This book has given me an opportunity to reflect on their invaluable contributions. My family, partner, team, friends—in fact, every person I have crossed paths with—has left a lasting impression and enriched my life in some way. While my name appears as the author of this book, it is undeniably a story of collective effort. I want to thank every single person from the bottom of my heart—you have all shaped me into who I am today.

Several others have worked tirelessly to ensure this book could come to life. A heartfelt thank you to Radhika Marwah and the team at Penguin Random House India, who believed in my story and went above and beyond to share it with the world.

Last but certainly not least, my deepest gratitude to Rinku Paul, who helped me articulate my thoughts and brought my story to life.

Scan QR code to access the
Penguin Random House India website